Praise for *Women Still at Work*

"Thanks to Liz Fideler for profiling 'our' cohort—middle-class women over 65 still at work. It's good to know that the graying of female professionals is no barrier to continued employment. I enjoyed reading about the interesting women Fideler introduces and learning how they manage their lives in and out of work." —**Sharon Feiman-Nemser**, Brandeis University

"Elizabeth F. Fideler tells the stories of older working women, backing them up with comparisons to national data and the latest research. Her stories are particularly compelling as they document the lives of a group of women who have been rejecting social norms all along the way, with working in retirement being the latest iteration." —**Jacquelyn B. James**, director of research, Sloan Center on Aging & Work; research professor, Boston College

"In exploring the phenomenon of older working women, Elizabeth Fideler weaves together substantive interviews and contemporary statistical data to create a very optimistic work. The strong, vibrant older women who shared their stories with Fideler are compelling examples of the benefits of staying on the job and 'off the shelf' in later life. While the high-powered women interviewed here are by no means typical, they provide wonderful examples of the importance of mentoring, persistence, and positivity for women who have the opportunities to stay active and engaged in the workplace well beyond modern thresholds of old age." —**Susannah Ottaway**, Carleton College

Women Still
at Work

Women Still at Work

Professionals over Sixty and on the Job

ELIZABETH F. FIDELER

ROWMAN & LITTLEFIELD PUBLISHERS, INC.
Lanham • Boulder • New York • Toronto • Plymouth, UK

Grateful acknowledgment is made for permission to reprint excerpts from the following copyrighted works:

From THE GRAPES OF WRATH by John Steinbeck, copyright 1939, renewed © 1967 by John Steinbeck. Used by permission of Viking Penguin, a division of Penguin Group (USA) Inc.

From THE ELEGANCE OF THE HEDGEHOG by Muriel Barbery. Used by permission of Europa Editions.

From DOING SIXTY AND SEVENTY by Gloria Steinem. Used by permission of Elders Academy Press.

From OUT WITH THE YOUNG AND IN WITH THE OLD: U.S. LABOR MARKETS 2000–2008 AND THE CASE FOR AN IMMEDIATE JOBS CREATION PROGRAM FOR TEENS AND YOUNG ADULTS by Andrew Sum, Joseph McLaughlin, et al. Used by permission of the Center for Labor Market Studies, Northeastern University.

From ENCORE, copyright © 2008 by Marc Freedman. Reprinted by permission of PublicAffairs, a member of the Perseus Books Group.

From Gail Sheehy, Preface to WOMEN ON THE FRONT LINES—MEETING THE CHALLENGE OF AN AGING AMERICA by Jessie Allen and Alan Pifer. Used by permission of Urban Institute Press.

From TRAVELING WITH POMEGRANATES by Sue Monk Kidd and Ann Kidd Taylor, copyright © 2009 by Sue Monk Kidd & Ann Kidd Taylor. Used by permission of Viking Penguin, a division of Penguin Group (USA) Inc.

Published by Rowman & Littlefield Publishers, Inc.
A wholly owned subsidiary of The Rowman & Littlefield Publishing Group, Inc.
4501 Forbes Boulevard, Suite 200, Lanham, Maryland 20706
www.rowman.com

10 Thornbury Road, Plymouth PL6 7PP, United Kingdom

British Library Cataloguing in Publication Information Available

Library of Congress Cataloging-in-Publication Data

Fideler, Elizabeth S., 1942-
  Women still at work : professionals over sixty and on the job / Elizabeth S. Fideler.
    p. cm.
  Includes bibliographical references.
  ISBN 978-1-4422-1550-4 (cloth : alk. paper) — ISBN 978-1-4422-1552-8 (ebook)
  1. Older women—Employment--United States. 2. Age and employment—United States. I. Title.
  HD6056.2.U6F53 2012
  331.4084'60973—dc23

                                                                    2012017802

∞™ The paper used in this publication meets the minimum requirements of American National Standard for Information Sciences—Permanence of Paper for Printed Library Materials, ANSI/NISO Z39.48-1992.

Printed in the United States of America

Contents

Acknowledgments

I am indebted to all 155 professional women who completed my survey, especially to the thirty-four spirited women who so generously gave of their time for an interview and those who forwarded the survey to other older working women around the country.

Many thanks are owed to colleagues and friends, including Ellie Slovis, Carol Grant, Barbara Resnek, Nancy Bills, Kathy Vassar, Deb Shanley, Allan Shedlin, Judy Perry, Cory Stebel, and David Freund, who helped keep the survey snowballing by passing it along to their colleagues and friends who are still on the job.

I am also very grateful to the following people who took an interest in my project early on and gave valuable advice at critical junctures: Dr. Jacquelyn B. James and the Sloan Center on Aging and Work, Dr. Charles V. Willie, Dr. John Collins III, Dr. Mary Coleman, Dr. Geraldine Brookins, Dr. Tatjana Meschede, Ralph Woodward, and the librarians at the Framingham Public Library.

To Sarah Stanton, my editor at Rowman & Littlefield, and Jin Yu, assistant editor, thanks for making the entire publishing process as smooth as it could be.

And to my dear husband, Dr. Paul A. Fideler, I offer my deepest appreciation for your willingness to listen and your unwavering support.

1

Introduction

Man, he lives in jerks—baby born an a man dies, an' that's a jerk—gets a
farm an' loses his farm, an' that's a jerk. Woman, it's all in one flow, like a
stream, little eddies, little waterfalls, but the river, it goes right on. Woman
looks at it like that.—Ma Joad, in John Steinbeck, *The Grapes of Wrath*

Ask anyone to name well-known older American women who are still working and you might hear about actress and comedienne Betty White, ninety
and guest host on *Saturday Night Live*; film, stage, and screen actress Lauren
Bacall, eighty-eight; cabaret and concert singer Barbara Cook, eighty-five;
poet and memoirist Maya Angelou, eighty-four; broadcast journalist and
television host Barbara Walters, eighty-three; author and professor Toni
Morrison, eighty-one; artist, musician, activist Yoko Ono, seventy-nine; Associate Justice of the Supreme Court Ruth Bader Ginsburg, seventy-nine; US
senators Dianne Feinstein and Barbara Boxer, seventy-nine and seventy-two,
respectively; stage, film, and television actress, dancer, singer Chita Rivera,
seventy-nine; Congresswoman Eleanor Holmes Norton, seventy-five; record-
ing artist Roberta Flack, seventy-five; activist and founder of the Children's
Defense Fund Marian Wright Edelman, seventy-three; former Speaker of the
House of Representatives Nancy Pelosi, seventy-two; journalist and foreign
correspondent Charlayne Hunter Gault, seventy; fashion model Lauren Hut-
ton, sixty-nine; Oscar-winning actress Meryl Streep, sixty-three; or actress,

playwright, professor Anna Deavere Smith, sixty-two. Active, smart, talented professionals, one and all. They are famous and deservedly so.

Not the least famous but decidedly active, smart, and talented are the many professional women who sail past age sixty, fly past sixty-five, and keep right on enjoying their work, making important contributions, each in their own way. They give short shrift to retirement, often because they enjoy their jobs and want to keep working. Sometimes the reasons to keep working are because of financial or familial circumstances or the need to hang onto health insurance coverage. They may work full time or part time; they may be self-employed or consulting. At the end of the day, for the most part, they simply love what they do. As one intrepid eighty-year-old caterer/cooking instructor/cookbook author told her daughter, "I will retire when they stop calling me!"

Then there are educated, experienced, competent older women who do not have a job but are still counted as labor force participants because they are actively looking for work. They do not want to retire, yet they are often sidelined. Numerous expressions describe how they are *put out to pasture, eased off into the sunset, written off,* or *put on the shelf. On the shelf* describes how a reluctantly unemployed _____ (fill in the blank) feels when un-employment benefits have terminated and job prospects are slim in a down economy, despite (or perhaps because of) an advanced degree. Its opposite *off the shelf* is far more positive. High tech firms, construction companies, and other businesses frequently decide to take programs, plans, proposals, and so on *off the shelf* because they are pretty much *ready to go.* They may need a bit of tweaking, but they can be put into action with minimal delay. It is far better to be *off* the shelf if you wish to be in the workforce.

Even someone who chooses retirement can experience feelings of loss and self-consciousness when out of the workforce. In her evocatively titled book *Groping toward Whatever or How I Learned to Retire [Sort Of]*, Susan Trausch describes how she had to learn to retire after her newspaper career spanning three decades at the *Boston Globe* came to an end, the fuzziness of her state of mind indicated by the words "sort of" appended in brackets to her main title. She admits to feeling "professionally naked" when asked what she does now that she's retired, even though she continues to write.[1] Although she was not laid off and was ready to accept the *Globe*'s buyout offer when it came her way, Trausch's sense of not belonging left her adrift. It took her a very long time to come to terms with being unemployed, and writing about the situation certainly helped her cope.

Women Still at Work: Professionals over Sixty and on the Job presents paradigmatic *real-life* older working women who, in the midst of the turmoil caused by the Great Recession and its aftermath, are holding their own in the paid workforce well beyond the point they might have retired. Demographic developments, primarily the two intersecting themes of *gender* and *age*, are colliding with current economic conditions to spark a new phenomenon: the fastest-growing cohort by rate of increase in the paid workforce is women sixty-five and older.[2] In addition, other equally important factors are influencing the timing of retirement for older women. *Women Still at Work* uncovers their reasons for opting to work and tells their stories, truly success stories in which older women workers are finally getting their due. When they came of age in the 1950s and 1960s, occupational options for young women were severely limited. Those women who have persevered, either in their original fields or in second and third careers, deserve to be celebrated not only for their staying power and what they contribute as workers but also for navigating so astutely during the recession.

My purpose is to explore the older working woman phenomenon by investigating what positions professional women hold in the paid workforce and where, plus the myriad reasons why they are still actively employed full time or part time when retirement and leisure beckon. After considering various social and policy influences and identifying the people who encouraged or inspired them to follow an early or later career path, I discuss personal challenges and concerns associated with juggling family caregiving and job responsibilities over many years and how older working women use what spare time they do have. These attributes and experiences are compared with statistical profiles drawn from the federal government's labor force projections, based on population growth and participation rate changes.

All this is set within the framework of the nationwide downturn that intensified between 2007 and 2009 and led to a flood of job losses, home foreclosures, bankruptcies, bank and investment company failures, taxpayer bailouts, and a credit crisis. Economic uncertainties on a national (and global) scale have caused financial insecurity on the personal level, and even those fortunate enough to have a job are not immune. When unemployment rises in forty-three states, something is terribly amiss.[3] When unemployment averages 10 percent in sixteen European Union countries, something is seriously amiss. When Harvard University has to tighten its belt and revise its ambitious expansion plans because of unprecedented losses to the largest university endowment in the country, well, you get the picture.

Housing prices have tumbled in most parts of the country and many homeowners owe more on their mortgages than their properties are worth. While median household wealth has declined for Americans in general, the collapse of the housing market has had a much greater impact on minorities than on whites. According to a Pew Foundation study using Census Bureau data, Hispanics, blacks, and Asians have been hit the hardest.[4]

During late 2011, some economic analysts were still saying a "double dip" is coming soon. Amid uncertainty about whether the Great Recession has actually ended, the *Wall Street Journal* reports that unemployment will remain elevated for years to come. The jobless rate hovered around 9.6 and 9.7 percent for months, dropped ever so briefly below 9.0, and then rose again to 9.2. Counting people who have stopped looking for work or are underemployed in part-time jobs, the more inclusive measure is 16.9 percent (totaling some 25 million). The average length of unemployment—more than thirty-one weeks—is at a record high and rising. According to the Pew Economic Policy Group, long-term unemployment is rife across industries and occupations and among men and women of all ages and educational backgrounds.[5] We once believed that postsecondary education provides protection against unemployment; once out of work, however, jobless people with higher education are likely to remain out of luck for extended periods. And while fewer workers fifty-five or older make up the overall unemployed population, those who are laid off in this age group are more likely to face protracted unemployment.[6]

Although the labor market is *said* to be recovering from its steep downturn, it could take as much as a decade to replace the 8 million-plus jobs that have been lost since December 2007.[7] As a consequence, unemployed older Americans are opting for early retirement in ever greater numbers. The Social Security Administration is seeing a surge in filing for benefits, particularly by hard-pressed sixty-two and sixty-three-year-olds whose unemployment checks have stopped coming.[8] Under the circumstances, it is remarkable to find older women participating in the labor market to an extent never seen before. Join me in investigating this unprecedented development.

Before we start, an explanation is in order. What initially triggered this national study of older women in the paid workforce was my personal struggle to adjust to a retirement I did not choose. A highly satisfying full-time job ended when my research grant ended and was followed by some consulting, some unemployment compensation, and many attempts to land a comparable new position. At the height of the Great Recession, getting a job for which I was not overqualified proved impossible, and, eventually, I found myself on the shelf against my wishes. Being curious (as well as educated, experienced, competent, and definitely older), I began to explore whether others were in the same situation and how the aforementioned demographic developments were colliding with current economic conditions, and the study began to take shape. Fortunately, too, at this time the Sloan Center on Aging and Work at Boston College invited me to become a research fellow, providing encouragement as well as a community of researchers with similar interests.

Data collection occurred in two phases between December 2009 and September 2011. First, I designed a survey that I sent to colleagues, friends, and friends of friends, asking them to refer or recruit other working women sixty or older who might be interested in participating in the project. This methodology, what sociologists call a "snowball sample," generated additional subjects and allowed me to gather information from 155 professional women with decades of work experience, virtually all well-educated high-achievers who still enjoy good health, and have a surprising amount of vigor and energy. Not only did the survey snowball, it went positively viral: responses came from all segments of the country and even from abroad. Remarkably, the survey traveled *via* e-mail from Michigan to Maryland to Cape Cod all the way to Dakar, Senegal, with one person recruiting another.

In the second phase, using a protocol that I developed, I conducted hour-long interviews (mostly by telephone and a few in person) of a subset of thirty-four women, or 22 percent of the survey respondents. The interviews allowed me to form a more complete picture of the respondents' lives, with a particular focus on their overall work experience and their attitudes toward retirement.

While the question of whether or not to retire comes up throughout the stories in this book, *Women Still at Work* is not a book about retirement. There are a number of excellent books on helping people decide when and how to retire, and offering suggestions as to how to find fulfillment in this stage of life. I recognize that retirement is a valid and long-sought after choice for many people. This book, however, focuses on the women who continue to work past traditional retirement age and tries to unravel the many reasons they make up this expanding segment of the US workforce, even during challenging economic times.

This study like any other has its parameters. The most obvious one— defining "older"—is discussed at length in chapter 3. For now my focus is age sixty and up, which is meant to include the oldest of the baby boomers and the younger oldsters, but not the oldest. Four other caveats require explanation.

First, the main focus of *Women Still at Work* is older women. Older men are addressed only insofar as they are accounted for in national population and labor market trends, the retirement research literature, and the profiles of individual women. What historians tell us about differences between older men and women in Western societies in past centuries seems to hold just as true today: they differ "in their social and work activities, their networks of kin and friends, and their self-fashioning."[9] Yet, when it comes to gender differences appearing in later-life labor force behavior and retirement, the mechanisms underlying identified differences are not well understood, say sociologists David Warner, Mark Hayward, and Melissa Hardy, at least in part because prior researchers have often studied work and retirement behavior of women using models developed on samples of men. In contrast, employing a "gendered life course perspective," Warner and his colleagues find substantial differences in the labor force behavior and retirement expectations of men and women, with early retirement more pronounced among women and late retirement less so. (They also note the "more tenuous labor force prospects" of blacks and Hispanics and their earlier exit from the workforce than whites and call for deeper understanding of the factors responsible for such differences in labor force transitions.)[10] However, while *Women Still at Work* responds to the call for greater insight into the mechanisms underlying the labor force behavior of older women, it does so with a surprising twist, for certain women are defying expectations by delaying retirement and we need to find out why this is so. Notwithstanding the specter of long-term unemployment, perhaps permanent joblessness, that is a real threat these days, especially for an older worker who is laid off or considering exit from the labor force for another reason, is that risk motivation enough to remain employed, or are other factors in play?

Second, for this study respondents had to be in the *paid* workforce. Women who serve in a purely voluntary capacity were not eligible. As a long-time member of the board of trustees of my local public library system and coordinator of our "one book, one community" initiative, I hasten to say that I have the highest regard for volunteer work and know that many working women perform valuable volunteer service in addition to their regular jobs.

Third, I acknowledge the relatively low representation of minority women in my research (8 percent), clearly a drawback of snowball sampling that does not extend throughout all social groups. Although my survey tapped into a wide spectrum of occupations and different geographical regions, it did not reach many nonwhite professional women with superior educational attainment and earning power. The survey circulated among friends and colleagues and occasionally from sister to sister, or sister-in-law, who typically were white women sharing similar socioeconomic status. Thus, with only modest diversity in terms of race and ethnicity, the survey findings cannot be generalized across the population of all older professional working women. Fortunately, the stories of the thirty-four women I interviewed suggest the considerable diversity to be found among older career women.

The fourth parameter is also related to socioeconomic status. Since the survey did not circulate among poorly educated older working women employed in low-wage, high turnover jobs, such as clerking in a retail store or supermarket, the sample does not represent the population of all older women workers. Although many of the older working women I studied can be described as privileged or even highly privileged, they did not all "come from money," as the saying goes, and all have worked hard to get to where they are today. Some people use the word *privileged* in a pejorative sense to connote elitism. While recognizing that my subjects were generally better off financially than most in their age group and continued to be above-average financially even during the protracted economic decline, I prefer to use the descriptor *privileged* in a positive sense to refer to how very fortunate they know they are to be able to *choose* between work and retirement.

Survey respondents' enthusiasm for the study was palpable and reinforced my belief that I had tapped into a rich seam of information about my age cohort—particularly what motivates them to keep working after thirty, forty, fifty or more years. Several women thanked me profusely for conducting this research. Many took the time to comment about how delighted they were to be asked what they were doing and why. One sixty-year-old university administrator penned an honest appraisal of the survey's effect on her: "This was a useful exercise if only to allow me to consider why I continue to work. I was surprised and pleased that I had so many reasons for staying in the work-force. At the same time, I can also see that I devote a *great deal of time* to my career. It will be interesting when I step out to see how I fare. Your research will be valuable for all of us women 'of a certain age' and those who look at employment policy and practice and gender equity!" As a result of answering the survey, another woman, a sixty-three-year-old full-time pharmaceutical salesperson, discovered something important about herself: "I did not realize that I still enjoy working so much!"

My curiosity about older women in the paid workforce, what they are do-ing, and why they are continuing to work in the context of a severe recession and its aftermath led me to explore this subject. I do not want to sound like a Pollyanna, but this is one ray of sunshine in an otherwise gloomy scenario. In contrast to common perceptions about older people—their physical prob-lems, their inability to keep up or learn new ways of doing things, and so on—the women I studied challenge such stereotypes. They are not merely career focused and hard working, they are also independent minded, well educated, healthy, energetic, spunky, prepossessing, persevering, and relatively com-fortable financially. Many are still struggling to achieve a satisfactory balance between work and life that can include more time with grandchildren and for enjoying their favorite leisure activities. Many possess a social conscience that reminds them to make time for helping those who are less fortunate or in need of guidance. I sincerely hope this book uncovers some valuable insights for my age peers as well as the enormous cohort of 77 million baby boomers following hard on our heels and the smaller cohort behind them. To that end, in the next chapter let's look at different philosophies and attitudes about women, aging, and retirement.

2

The Realities of Work and Aging in America

Always remember that there's a retirement home waiting somewhere
and so we have to surpass ourselves every day, make every day undying.
Climb our own personal Everest and do it in such a way that every step is a
little bit of eternity.—Muriel Barbery, *The Elegance of the Hedgehog*

I am not suggesting that aging is all roses. Far from it. Many senior women admit to feeling or looking older, or out of touch because their clothing may be out of fashion or the wrong length. Their hairstyles and coloring are not bold or sexy. Their tastes in music and television shows are not cutting edge. They still use a landline and an answering machine, and might have e-mail. (Re landlines: a *New Yorker* cartoon that I saved depicts two middle-aged women chatting in a cupcake store, one telling the other that she knows her gentleman friend is very stable because he has a landline. Re e-mail: my husband and I have to remind one of our texting-only teenaged grandsons to check his e-mail once in a while to see if there is a message from his grandparents.) Seniors are said to be uncomfortable with new, fast-paced technologies, such as instant messaging, texting, tweeting, Facebook, and YouTube.[1] The television remote (also known as the clicker) may baffle them if something goes awry. (I speak from experience.) They are old enough to have grandchildren and maybe even great-grands. Everyone at work is likely to be much, much younger (and the doctors they see are often younger than their children).

They have lived through events that younger folks either know nothing about or are considered to be "ancient history."

On the flip side, there are many advantages to aging. A friend e-mailed a tongue-in-cheek list to me that was circulating around the country on humor websites unattributed. Here are several truly mordant "facts":

- No one expects you to run—anywhere.
- People call at 9 p.m. and ask, "Did I wake you?"
- There is nothing left to learn the hard way.
- Things you buy now will not wear out.
- You can eat supper at 4 p.m.
- You can live without sex but not your glasses.
- Your eyes will not get much worse.
- Your investment in health insurance is finally beginning to pay off.
- Your joints are more accurate meteorologists than the National Weather Service.
- Your secrets are safe with your friends because they can't remember them either.

As funny as these "facts" may be, it is important to acknowledge that they also perpetuate negative stereotypes about aging that can feed into discrimination in the workplace and can even undermine the cognitive or physical health of seniors who denigrate themselves because of them.

To give them their due, older folks are apt to have acquired much wisdom and patience over the years and an ability to take the long view of situations. Gail Sheehy proposes that we learn from vital, energetic, creative postmenopausal women over fifty whom she calls "wisewomen." They are "transformative figures" who "live their passions."[2] Such women are very special, but fortunately they are not exceedingly rare. Steinbeck's Ma Joad, the pillar of her benighted Okie family, comes readily to mind; likewise a mature, second-career, African American inner-city teacher I once got to know who referred to the wisdom and insightfulness she and her friends possessed as "mother wit." Senior women have much mother wit to offer the generations coming up behind them, if anyone will listen.

When I was a young mother with two toddlers, I eagerly gathered tips from slightly older but more experienced women raising children. Now, once again, I am recognizing the value in learning from the experiences of those around me and ahead of me. Ideally, baby boomers and the cohorts behind them, responding to the social and economic conditions specific to their own times, will also benefit from examples set by and experiences of today's older working women.

For example, age encourages taking the long view of situations. A wise-woman develops an awareness of and capacity to live with life's complexities.[3] This awareness was illustrated for me during a recent exchange at a book club meeting when my friends and I were discussing Elizabeth Strout's Pulitzer Prize-winning novel, *Olive Kitteridge*. I was struck by the honest self-appraisal shared by an over-seventy-year old friend who said something to the effect of: "In my younger years everything was black or white, right or wrong. Now I can see and appreciate the grays, the different sides of a situation." And although Olive Kitteridge did not see the error of her ways until too late, my friend knows she is glad to be more open-minded now.

An altogether different type of awareness comes with age-creep and, associated with that, health scares and physical limitations. Time is marching on. Use it or lose it. The future is now. Gloria Steinem underscores this point: "Whether we are eighty or eight, everything is present in the Now."[4] Active older women can help the next generations "fill in the blank screen of imagined futures" and serve as "personal role models of living in the present."[5] In the same vein, one of the formidable females Sheehy interviewed declared that she wanted to live "as long as I can be useful, especially to other women."

If the future is now, why not start a new business or career, build houses with Habitat for Humanity, or run for legislative office? Or, on a more frivolous note (germane nonetheless), if you have been saving your mother's or grandmother's best china for special occasions for years and years as so many women have, why not use it? I have given myself permission to take the precious place settings out of their boxes and protective cases. And, oh yes, *my* newest venture is writing a book that can be useful to other women.

Workers have long fought for the right to retire with dignity, and I recognize that it can be an optimal choice for many people. However, there are also many reasons for not heeding the beckoning call of retirement and taking one's ease. Some people are convinced that life falls apart when you retire. An example close to home: my step-mother married her third husband after my father died. Eddie was a warm, gregarious man who never stopped going every weekday to his office in the city and who played golf on weekends until he passed away after heart surgery at the age of ninety. When he was still in his eighties and I politely tried to ask him whether he contemplated retirement, he shot back with, "Never!" The reason: Each of his business partners over the years had died soon after retiring, and Eddie wanted none of it.

Things can fall apart in less extreme but nonetheless difficult ways. Many workers are reconsidering retirement in view of economic uncertainties. In 2007 (*well before* the recession hit hard, the stock market plunged, and retirement savings shriveled) nearly half of the three thousand baby boomers responding to a *Money* magazine survey said they were not able to save enough to maintain their standard of living in retirement. About 70 percent wanted to continue working, even if they did not need to for financial reasons.[6] The very next year with the recession in full force, a McKinsey Global Institute survey revealed that 85 percent of boomers are likely to continue working beyond the traditional retirement age, and two out of three of the oldest boomers are financially unprepared for retirement.[7] Employers were saying the same thing about the same time, the Center for Retirement Research at Boston College confirms: a survey of four hundred nationally representative employers found that respondents expect half their employees over age fifty to lack sufficient resources for retirement at the traditional retirement age for their organization, and half of those employees without sufficient resources for retirement will plan to work (with the same or a different employer) at least two years longer than was true of workers in the past.[8]

No wonder that, owing to the poor economy, prospects for retirement have become even bleaker. An annual Retirement Confidence Survey by the Employee Benefit Research Institute finds that American workers of all ages have lost confidence regarding having enough to retire comfortably (only 13 percent are very confident). Among workers ages fifty-five and up confidence has declined steadily since 1999, sinking in 2011 to the lowest level ever measured by the survey in its twenty-one-year history. Therefore, workers of all ages expect to work longer, especially to boost their financial security: 74 percent said they will supplement their income in retirement *by working for pay* (compared to 70 percent in 2010 and 66 percent in 2007).[9] The Sloan Center on Aging and Work at Boston College dubs working in retirement "the new normal" and "a 21st century phenomenon."[10]

Anne O'Sullivan is one of the growing cohort of older women who are working in retirement. Hers is an "encore career"[11] that generates income and has a social impact.

PROFILE: ANNE O'SULLIVAN

In 2000 when she was sixty-eight, Anne O'Sullivan retired and relocated to Vermont. Long an avid skier, she was drawn to Mt. Snow and by the opportunity to volunteer as a Mountain Ambassador at the big mountain resort. Ambassadors in bright yellow and blue jackets provide service to Mt. Snow's guests and staff in exchange for a season pass and other perks. However, after a few years of leisure, when her landlord increased the rent and she needed a new car, Anne realized with a start that she would have to go back to work. Having been divorced for many years, she was entirely on her own. "Work came as quite a surprise after retirement," she admits. "The impetus was altogether financial. I was already in my seventies, for goodness sake!"

With doctoral work and extensive management experience in different settings under her belt, Anne was confident she could fit in almost anywhere. She answered an ad in the local Deerfield Valley newspaper and was hired for part-time project evaluation work by the director of a drug and alcohol prevention coalition in Wilmington. The town had received one of twenty-three Vermont Department of Health grants aimed at developing, strengthening, and maintaining substance abuse prevention services throughout the state. Under a five-year grant from the US Department of Health and Human Services, the state agency aimed to intervene before substance abuse could become a life-long problem for youth, young adults, their parents, and the community. Soon another drug and alcohol prevention coalition based in Bennington also hired Anne to be a part-time project evaluator.

Over the course of three years Anne attended several state agency training sessions for coalition staff across the state which helped provide a context for her work. Although her official title is project evaluator, Anne does many other things, such as writing the coalition newsletter. "I am a jack of all trades and can usually fill in where needed." She rates herself as "pretty good" on the computer, using e-mail, creating Excel spreadsheets, and managing the software for setting up the newsletter. Facebook and texting are not for her. Anne also heads a suicide prevention project for one of the coalitions (suicide being the second leading cause of death among eleven to twenty-two-year-olds in the state). The project is connected to school-based suicide prevention programs, and her focus is coaching community leaders and first responders. Grant funding is administered by the Center for Health and Learning, a private nonprofit organization that contracts with the State of Vermont Department of Health.

The major focus in Anne's life at present is her family of five children and seventeen grandchildren who live all over the country. She takes immense pleasure in interacting with her mostly grown up grandkids. "It is important to keep my work life within reasonable bounds so I can be available to them. I do not let work consume my life as it did when I was younger." In the past, Anne was New York State's Deputy Commissioner for Quality Assurance in the Office of Mental Health following work as the Director for Quality Assurance in two of New York's mental health facilities. Later in her career, she became executive director of the international arm of an organization called RSVP (Retired Service Volunteers Program). She traveled all over the world setting up and advising RSVP programs in many countries. Now, at age seventy-eight, except for visits to see her extended family, Anne prefers to be a "homebody."

Not only has her attitude toward travel changed, her reasons for working have changed as well. Anne puts loyalty to the job, her colleagues, and the coalition's clients first (though finances are always a strain and the money is always welcome). "At my age I am in an enviable position: I am no longer trying to climb the career ladder. There is no ego involvement. I am completely done with all that. I have no axe to grind and I can speak up honestly about management and personnel issues. It actually makes me much more valuable."

When asked how long she intends to keep working, Anne replies, "I will continue working so long as the funding holds out. The recession has exacerbated the problem of securing grant funding for nonprofit organizations like ours."

Anne has friends in different age groups, mostly in their fifties and sixties, who are still working. "People assume that I am ten to fifteen years younger than I really am, even with the gray hair. Everyone at work is younger. Although society as a whole writes off people with gray hair, I have had no problem with ageism at work." On the other hand, having been very athletic all her life, Anne is currently experiencing some worrisome health concerns. This year will be the first time she does not plan to ski because of recurring muscle aches and pains that threaten to sideline her. Not to be deterred, and as a believer in preventive measures, she participates in RSVP bone builders class, walks, and does yoga.

Anne's philosophy is: Do not take on things that have a steep learning curve or a twenty-four-hour deadline. Avoid anything that induces a lot of stress. "Since I can do my work at home most of the time, I have a lot of control over my time and can easily fit everything in—work, leisure, friends, and family." She takes adult learning classes. She volunteers as a driver when Deerfield Valley Transportation needs her to take people to their hospital, doctor, and dental appointments. The opportunity to meet new and different people is a benefit of this volunteer work. In addition, Anne is on the Wilmington Beautification Committee and the Affordable Housing Committee. Advocacy for senior housing is her particular interest.

At this stage in her life, Anne is grateful to have good friends she can count on. She thinks of them as a mutual aid society. "I have several really close male friends who are very important to me and who often step in when I am in need of help. My women friends are especially crucial as confidants and supporters. They are in my life on a daily basis. My family is scattered and busy with their own lives, and I do not know what I would do without my friends."

In contrast to professional men of her generation who tend to be defined by their work, are accustomed to taking charge, and often dread losing their identity when they retire, Anne has moved gracefully out of the executive roles she once held. Working in retirement was not what she originally planned, but it works beautifully for her.

The Families and Work Institute (FWI) conducts research on US workers' lives on and off the job. FWI conducts its "National Study of the Changing Work Force" every five years with a large nationally representative sample of US workers. Recent analysis of data from the FWI study found that three-quarters of survey respondents fifty and older who had not yet retired expected to work once they were retired.[12]

Along parallel lines, deferred retirement is becoming an ever more practical choice. Selected data from 1999 and 2009 EBRI Retirement Confidence Surveys show far fewer baby boomers and older workers wanting to retire at sixty-five, compared with respondents of the same ages a decade earlier (18 percent of boomers in 2009 compared with 34 percent in 1999; 15 percent of workers fifty-five and older in 2009 compared with 28 percent in 1999). There was a sharp increase in both groups saying they plan to postpone retirement until age sixty-six *or higher* (boomers: 35 percent compared with 20 percent a decade earlier; older workers: 34 percent compared with 20 percent a decade earlier). No doubt some workers' preference for a later retirement can be attributed to the hike in the age for collecting full Social Security benefits.[13] Some workers said they will *never* retire (boomers: 13 percent saying this compared with 5 percent earlier; older workers: 11 percent saying this compared with 8 percent earlier).[14]

Similarly, the National Institute on Retirement Security says that, as a direct result of the economic downturn, 83 percent of Americans in 2009 were concerned about their ability to retire.[15] Clearly, the economic crisis has sent a "wake-up call" that is changing some behaviors and causing workers to reset views and develop new priorities. Consequently, as one popular columnist advises, the best remedy for retirement security may simply be not to retire: working longer is a practical solution for those in good health and already in higher income brackets.[16] By the year 2018, owing to good health and various economic incentives, participation of seniors sixty-five and older in the labor force is projected to grow nearly ten times faster than the total labor force (a 78 percent increase compared to 8 percent).[17] Put another way, the same age group is expected to account for 6.1 percent of the total labor force by 2016, a spike of 2.5 percentage points in ten years.[18] Even as of 2011 when labor participation rates for seniors were clearly trending upward, the most dramatic increases were attributable to women workers. And the better educated seniors are, the more likely they are to still be at work and in higher-paying jobs (management, professional, and related occupations). Thus, not everyone is prospering. The overall labor force participation rate of older Americans (age fifty-five and up) across all races and ethnicities grew from 29.4 percent in 1993 to 40.2 percent in 2010; yet 2009 saw an interruption in the growth pattern with participation rates declining for blacks and Hispanics, particularly men hit hardest by the worsening job market, while holding on for whites and Asian older workers.[19]

In October 2009 *Time* magazine declared women more anxious than men about financial security, as the recession "raises the stakes and shuffles the deck." [20] *Time* went on to forecast "an extraordinary change in a single generation." For the first time in history the majority of US workers would be females, mainly because males have been hit harder by the downturn and by the disappearance of jobs requiring physical strength. *Time* offered a corollary: women are more frequently the primary breadwinners in their households. Within a few short months, in January 2010 the Labor Department had indeed confirmed that women held more than 50 percent of nonfarm payroll jobs (women 50.3 percent, men 49.7 percent). While the deep downturn has hurt both men and women, men have been losing jobs nearly twice as fast as women. The Labor Department explains that jobs held by men tend to be in industries that fluctuate seasonally and are sensitive to the economic cycle, while women tend to work in "safer" fields such as government, health care, and education that are less susceptible to business or seasonal cycles.[21]

A more intangible but no less compelling reason older women may choose to buck convention by continuing in the paid workforce is their sense of empowerment and vitality. To be sure, not all older women were feminists back in the day. Not all have ideological motives for continuing to work. Not all postmenopausal women are deliberately challenging the old stereotypes associated with aging and retirement. However, whether an activist or merely a bystander in past decades, any woman now in her sixties, seventies, or eighties was undoubtedly bombarded by powerful messages of the feminist movement.

I knew my book project had struck a feminist chord when I received the following impassioned missive from Margaret Gaston:

> Perhaps one reason for our ardor in participating in this project relates to how hard it has been for our cohort to (finally) participate fully in work within a professional community. Remember the early "mommy wars," fights for equal pay for equal work (OK, maybe we still have not seen the end of that one), the "glass ceiling" and other battles?
>
> The wonderful young women whom I know best—my daughter, daughter-in-law, and daughter-in-law to be—have little experience with the admonitions

we faced that we weren't qualified for this or not suited for that. They don't seem to have to surmount the same barriers we faced or be limited to choosing between a few female-friendly occupations for their life's work.

Maybe we are holding on because it was so damn hard to get here. My former doctor threw this question at me: Margaret, when are you going to put your fist down? This question was asked, of course, within the context of retirement and in reference to the many fights in which we all are engaged—civil rights, rights for all children to receive a good education, rights for women to have control over their own bodies, rights for women to choose their own career path, the right to good health care. The answer? Never!

When you read Margaret's profile, you will see that she has not put her fist down, even as she adjusts to professional and personal changes.

PROFILE: MARGARET GASTON

What Margaret Gaston humorously refers to as "The Last Lap" is an exciting time of transition for her. The president and chief executive officer of the Santa Cruz–based Center for the Future of Teaching and Learning and a California girl through and through, at age sixty-two she is accompanying her husband to Washington, D.C., where he has taken a new job. Despite the move to the East Coast, Margaret looks forward to continuing as the center's president and senior policy advisor. Margaret feels compelled to keep working toward the goal of ensuring that California has an adequate number of teachers in the employment pool, teachers who are well prepared and effective in the classroom, regardless of the route they take. "Every child is entitled to an effective teacher, not just those youngsters who reside in affluent communities."

After college and a master's degree, Margaret was an elementary classroom teacher and a high school vice principal before serving as a consultant and administrator for the California Department of Education, overseeing school reform efforts. She was later appointed by the governor to the California Commission on Teacher Credentialing where she served as the Commission's vice chair and chair of the legislative committee. In the 1990s she opened a private consulting firm from her mountainside ranch in Santa Cruz, advising foundation program officers, presidents, and boards on grant making to public education and education support entities on behalf of children and youth. Armed with the recommendations of the influential National Commission on Teaching and America's Future, Margaret met with key members of the California policy community, state legislators, researchers, and educators to explore ways that schools could improve student academic achievement. Having attained unanimous consensus that the quality of the teacher work force was central to their efforts, in 1995 Margaret won the support of the Stuart and Hewlett Foundations to establish the public, not-for-profit Center for the Future of Teaching and Learning which would be dedicated to the strengthening of teacher development policy and practice in California. She offered to help get the center up and running—establish a board, obtain non-profit status, hire an executive director—then she planned to return to her private practice (she had a young child at home at the time). Seventeen years later, she is still on board, having acquired the title president and executive director, contributing to the improvement of public education by using the impressive trove of knowledge and experience she has accumulated.

In the belief that sustained educational improvement will occur only when every student in every classroom has a fully prepared and effective teacher, the center shares a special interest in and commitment to improving learning conditions in high-poverty, low-performing schools across the state. The knowledge and skills of teachers are key to increasing students' academic achievement and, therefore, should be the foundation of any effort to improve public education. Thus, the strategic purpose of the center is to strengthen California's teacher workforce to deliver a rigorous and balanced curriculum for all students, thereby supporting every child's continued intellectual, ethical, and social development. "It is a 120 percent job. Keeping teacher quality on the front burner and overseeing a suite of products and services involves a lot of plate spinning," Margaret says frankly.

One center effort entails boosting the academic achievement of children and youth in foster care. Another initiative in partnership with the Lawrence Hall of Science at University of California, Berkeley, and others, puts a statewide focus on science teaching and learning. "It is ironic, given the rhetoric about our country's needs in STEM (science, technology, engineering, and mathematics), how the federal No Child Left Behind legislation has resulted in a narrowed curriculum—science has gone begging," Margaret observes. Other current center priorities are school leadership at the school site and district levels, an area about which too little is known, and ensuring that California has a high-quality teacher data system that is user-friendly. The center is making data on teaching and learning readily available on its website for all who seek access, not just academic researchers. "We are here to provide clear, reliable information and impartial advice re policy and practice to the governor, legislature, superintendent of public instruction, agency heads, journalists, philanthropic organizations, parents, and others interested in public education in California—not to advocate for or against individual bills."

Margaret's immediate goal is personal: to settle in the Washington, D.C., area where she and her husband, Dr. Robert M. Kaplan, are about to move. They are leaving behind their home in Pacific Grove, "a quiet little town that time forgot and the recession has devastated." This major change is occurring because Bob has just been appointed as director of the Office of Behavioral and Social Sciences Research (OBSSR) at the National Institutes of Health and NIH Associate Director for Behavioral and Social Sciences Research. OBSSR's work focuses on how behavioral and social factors often influence illness and health, such as tobacco-induced lung disease. The office stimulates and integrates behavioral and social sciences research across NIH's institutes and centers to improve the understanding, treatment, and prevention of disease. Dr. Kaplan has been the distinguished professor of the Department of Health Services in the School of Public Health and distinguished professor in the Department of Medicine at University of California/Los Angeles, is a member of the Institute of Medicine of the National Academies of Science, and is listed by Thompson Reuters web of knowledge as one of most cited scientific authors in the world.

"Our move is taking up all the air in the room right now!" Margaret laughs. When she and Bob married two years ago they formed a "blended" family. Their three grown children plus one spouse are all in graduate school and they are looking forward to welcoming a new daughter-in-law into the family in May. "They are wonderful young people just coming into their own. They are compassionate, caring, and funny, too. We are enjoying the fruits of our labors." They are a very active couple who go hiking and backpacking in the High Sierras. Margaret also enjoys horseback riding and does yoga three times a week. "At sixty-two, I do not take my health for granted. With the usual accumulation of age-related ills, I make sure to exercise every morning before work without fail. I have always been an outdoorsy person. It gives me pleasure and allows me to think through knotty problems!" Calling this phase of life "The Last Lap" has positive connotations for her: many women her age are enjoying resources and opportunities not previously available to older women, and they are thriving. "If I can stay healthy and intellectually active, I will be able to do the work I love."

Her longer term goal is professional: to help rebalance the mismatch between the needs of the public schools and the resources available to them. "We expected the teacher retirement wave to stabilize, especially during the recession when people were lucky to have a job to hold onto, but that is not what is happening in California. The boomers are retiring, even in this economy, just when we are seeing a new surge in elementary school enrollments. At the same time, we are experiencing a 50 percent drop in the number of novice teachers in the classroom, the number of applicants to teacher preparation programs has fallen, and the number of credentialed teachers has declined."

When incoming Governor Jerry Brown announced California's "tough budget for tough times," he was not exaggerating. His state has a staggering structural deficit of some $28 billion. The schools are caught in a squeeze: although the state can finally claim to have higher expectations for and greater scrutiny of student and teacher performance, resources intended to enable them to reach these goals are rapidly declining—education funding has decreased by $20 billion over the past three years alone. The center's annual inventory of teacher supply and demand shows that the teacher force is shrinking and classrooms are overcrowded, despite legislation authorizing class size reduction. Schools are closing, courses are eliminated, and staff are laid off. All is not bleak, however. Recent "omnibus" education bills are helping to correct the maldistribution of underprepared teachers in the lowest-performing schools and providing mentoring support for interns while they work toward credentialing. A new teacher performance assessment system is evaluating and supporting teacher candidates as they progress through their training, the state's novice teacher assessment frames professional development for the first two years in the classroom, and the National Board for Professional Teaching Standards certification process provides the high-end anchor for accomplished teaching. The goal of this assessment system is to strengthen teaching practice at different stages along the career continuum.

With all these challenges, Margaret is busier than ever. Not only is retirement out of the question, it is also being redefined by this true baby boomer. Margaret feels that retirement is quite different today. People are going about it in new ways, rejecting the vaunted move to a place beside the golf course. She cites her dearest friend, for instance, who retired and immersed herself in the arts, took on a half marathon, and travels widely. Margaret continues,

> The retirement question has changed for our generation because employment has become our life's work. It is a deep pleasure, honor, and privilege to carry out our responsibilities in the everyday world. I simply cannot imagine that caring for children would not be reflected in my work in the future, even if the shape, tenor, or depth of it changes over time. As I transition through different ways of working, I hope to take advantage of what I have experienced and apply what wisdom I have acquired to new and more complex sets of circumstances. Kids are still coming to school unprepared and struggling to learn to read. For example, let's find out whether we can use technology to bridge cultural divides and overcome the effects of poverty.

Moving and changing. Will she achieve a more satisfactory balance between work and family and leisure when she transitions to part-time status? "I really doubt it," says Margaret. "My work is very consuming, and I have not slain that dragon yet!"

In "Books as Bombs" commentator Louis Menand credits Betty Friedan with identifying "the problem that has no name" for apparently comfortable and economically secure women and giving it a name: *The Feminine Mystique*.[22] Whether Friedan was truly the first, whether she oversimplified and left out working class and minority women, the book did help to put gender (in)equality on the "public's radar screen" and resonated perfectly with the dissatisfactions of zillions of housewives who had been told to get an education and take a job in order to land a husband.

Davi-Ellen Chabner's story illustrates the early 1960s feminist mind-set especially well. After marriage and child rearing, she combined a good education, a desire to help others, the ability to pinpoint what would be useful, and her formidable drive and resourcefulness into what became a serious and highly satisfying career. Could she retire and rest on her considerable laurels? Sure. Would she? Most certainly not. She is still making her mark.

PROFILE: DAVI-ELLEN CHABNER

"Serendipitous" is the word sixty-six-year-old Davi-Ellen Chabner uses to describe her career trajectory as a teacher and author. Girls of her generation and mine were advised to get a good education then a husband, and she did follow those instructions . . . to a point. She excelled in the life sciences and English at Wellesley College, got married, earned a master of arts in teaching at Harvard Graduate School of Education, and had two children. But she was restless. "I saw my husband building his career in medicine at the NIH and I wanted to use my education, too. I yearned for an independent career alongside of marriage and raising children. I also wanted to do something significant to help others. Tennis dates did not satisfy that need and neither did shopping. The quote beneath my high school yearbook picture said that I was a 'crusader for rights,' and that was prophetic. Civil rights, women's rights, reproductive rights, sexual preference rights, immigration rights—I have taken them all on at one time or another!"

With consciousness-raising groups proliferating everywhere in the sixties and seventies, Davi embraced women's lib. She also started teaching biology part time at an alternative school for unwed teenage mothers. She quickly discovered that her students did not know the first thing about reproduction and birth control. At the same time, she discovered that she positively loved teaching. "I was really good at explaining things to people and a bit of an actress. I found my calling. Had I been born ten years later, I would have gone to medical school, but I am glad I threw myself into teaching." Davi interviewed for jobs in the Montgomery County School System in Maryland, but it was a human resources person from the NIH who called to invite her to offer a course in medical terminology for allied health personnel, such as medical assistants and nurse's aides. And then Montgomery College hired her as an adjunct to do the same.

There were no computers or copy machines in those days, only typewriters, carbon paper, and mimeograph machines. Davi spent a lot of time developing her own materials, as there were simply no adequate medical terminology textbooks available. Her husband's medical knowledge was a big help. In the belief that student writing is the best way to learn, she created original exercises, activities, pronunciation guides, and tests. "The classroom was my laboratory. When students would come to class with questions, I made sure to include that information on a worksheet." Before long, her department chair at the college took note and told Davi, "This would make a good book." Serendipity.

Gathering her courage, Davi contacted publishers. One acquisitions editor hustled her, grandly insisting that the book would make millions. That was not her goal. "When a representative of W.B. Saunders contacted me, we really clicked. In fact, we are still good friends after all these years. She offered a highly favorable contract with a percentage of the gross, though at the time I did not have the faintest idea of how favorable it was." The first edition of *The Language of Medicine* was born in 1976. Now more than 1,000 pages and in its tenth edition, the comprehensive workbook-text was followed by *Medical Terminology: A Short Course* (a sixth edition is under way), an abbreviated, introductory version of the longer workbook-text; and *Medical Language Instant Translator* (now in the fourth edition), a handy pocket-size reference guide to medical abbreviations, diagnostic tests and procedures, images of body parts, and the like. "It all keeps evolving. There are new technologies, interactive CDs, online courses. I realized a while ago that I can't do it all myself, so I work closely with my editor and others who have the technical know-how."

Men and women training for careers in hospitals and insurance companies, often at community colleges, use the books. Ironically, they are selling better than ever as more people are going into training because of the economic downturn and negative employment picture. What's more, Davi's books have been translated into Japanese, Korean, Chinese, and Russian. Grateful students from all over the world write to tell her that she has helped to change their lives, and other medical terminology instructors contact her for advice.

Her reasons for continuing to work hard are easy to fathom. Publishing has proved unusually lucrative, but more than the income it is the satisfaction she gets from interacting with new students every semester and the pride that comes from knowing that her books are making a difference. "I have been very fortunate. Being self-employed gives me time for my work and for my other passions—family first, my dogs, gym workouts, Pilates, yoga, photography, and travel with my husband. It has also enabled me to give something back and help others who are less fortunate." After she and her husband moved to Boston, she became a volunteer mentor in the Goodwill Industries after-school program for inner-city girls and was invited to serve on the boards of the Boston Conservatory and the Friends of the Massachusetts General Hospital Cancer Center.

When I mention the word "retirement," Davi insists she will keep working forever, or as long as she is healthy. She is a breast cancer survivor. "Illness came as a huge shock fifteen years ago, but I got through it with help from Bruce and my kids and, when we moved to the Boston area, I started marathoning. I was actually afraid to stop running (after nine Boston marathons on behalf of pediatric cancer patients at MGH and one in New York City), but when I turned sixty-five, I decided it was the right time and the right decision. Now I am into yoga! I have to do something physical every day."

It is only fair to tell you that Davi and I are old friends from high school and I have known her husband, a highly respected oncologist, almost as long. Ever since I first met her she has impressed me with the intensity, enthusiasm, and dedication she brings to activities she cares about the most. When she tells me that she drives from Boston to the Bronx occasionally to substitute for her daughter, an MD, who teaches Davi's medical terminology course at Lehman College, I am more amused than surprised. When she tells me that she has sponsored six deserving music and theater students from the United States, China, Bulgaria, and Poland at the Boston Conservatory over the past eight years, I understand how much it means to *her*, let alone those students. "Most people see retirement as a time to enjoy themselves and judge their happiness by the trips they take, their golf game, and so on. For Bruce and me, the work we do is not just a job. More than monetary rewards, it is being able to do what we love to do. As long as you have the passion and can help others, do not let age stop you. The number does not mean anything!"

I really do not think Davi's career trajectory can be explained by mere serendipity. Rather, I think she has had the wit and the pluck to make good things happen and the generous heart for spreading it around. And that is Davi for you, ever the crusader.

Feminism was hardly the only movement to spur social change in America of course. Other inequalities finally began to be confronted during the civil rights era. Activists and legislators broke new ground in the spheres of education, employment, and housing, among others, providing opportunities for people of color. One courageous young woman who helped to desegregate Little Rock's Central High School went on to become the impressive career woman described in the next profile. She sees her continuing work as important to furthering the cause of social justice.

PROFILE: SYBIL JORDAN HAMPTON

Sybil Jordan Hampton knows all about breaking new ground. Growing up in Little Rock, Arkansas, in the 1940s and 1950s, she drank at colored water fountains and attended segregated schools. Then in 1959 she was recruited to be a member of the second group of pioneering black students to integrate Central High School after the Little Rock Nine. Her younger brother was recruited for the queue that followed. At Central she was shunned by the white students and denied participation (by state law) in all extracurricular activities. Painful as it was for the sociable teenager to be isolated by her peers on a daily basis, she knew she did not deserve to be treated as a nonentity. Her parents, who were college educated and active in the National Association for the Advancement of Colored People (NAACP), reminded her not to take it personally. "It is not about you. If they knew you, they would love you!"

Her parents "believed that somebody had to go through the fire first and that change would never happen until there were people who were willing to step out and be on the front line." Furthermore, "there were experiences and relationships in my day-to-day life that reinforced my sense that we were good people and that we had worth." [23] Indeed, her teachers treated her well and the African Methodist Episcopal (AME) church community nurtured her. "My church was a breeding ground for responsible citizens, such as future teachers who would go on to do well and make things better for the race." In that era when Jim Crow was being challenged, it seemed like "one little drop in a big, big bucket, but I was blessed to have people feel the spark in me." Going to Central proved to be a pivotal experience.

Sybil graduated and went on to earn a bachelor's degree from Earlham College, a master's from the University of Chicago, and a doctorate in higher education from Teachers College, Columbia University. She was fortunate to be part of the generation of young black men and women for whom opportunities finally were available. And, throughout a forty-one-year career in the fields of philanthropy and higher education, she had several mentors who helped to keep the spark alive.

A notable accomplishment of Sybil's was serving as president of the Winthrop Rockefeller Foundation from 1996 to 2006. Upon assuming her responsibilities, she worked with the foundation board on assessing its capacity to respond to opportunities and challenges; strategic planning; and clarifying criteria and processes for grant decision making. She traveled around the state to learn firsthand what communities wanted and needed and where philanthropic dollars could make the biggest difference. The board retained two of the foundation's traditional foci—public education (particularly early childhood education) and economic development across Arkansas and in the Mississippi Delta. A third funding priority was added—economic, racial, and social justice.

Sybil and the foundation board endeavored to broaden understanding of social justice issues in Arkansas beyond the black/white continuum, for example, by telling the story of the Japanese internment camps set up in the southeastern part of the state during World War II and how Arkansans responded to the injustice and discrimination internees experienced. "I may not talk about race very much, because I have become aware that in Arkansas race is much too narrow a lens. My goal is that every child—every person—has the opportunity to become the best that he or she can be. Certainly I see things through the lens of race, but having once been isolated myself, I am careful to observe that there are lots of people who are hurt and who suffer because nobody stands up for them."[24]

Sybil decided to step down from the foundation presidency in 2006 to be more available to her mother who lives next door and has Alzheimer's. "I had to get off the road so I could be there more fully for her, yet I still wanted to keep working in order to provide optimal care for my mother and to pursue my lifelong passion for economic, racial, and social justice." Now, at sixty-seven and still energetic and resourceful, she is a consultant on a part-time basis, using her skills and experience to provide program development support, for example, to the Mississippi Teacher Corps program that provides out of classroom learning opportunities for high school youth in rural communities, under the auspices of the Atlanta-based Southern Education Foundation.

While the economic downturn has made consulting challenging, the rhythm of consulting work consists of stops and starts anyway. As a consultant must, she works from home and away from home. As often as possible, she and her husband exercise together at a senior center four nights a week to keep fit. He also "retired" in 2006 and is teaching mathematics at a local, historically black college.

Sybil does consulting work not only to be able to support her mother but also because "there is so much to be done. It is a joy to be able to choose what I do. When one is vibrant and sound of mind and body, it is imperative to continue to 'fight the good fight.' My husband teaches because he is committed to enabling youth at the margins to do well and be contributing members of this society. We, of course, need to work in these economically challenging times. Yet, we work at things we love and would do so under other circumstances."

With more flexibility in her life now, Sybil also devotes time to volunteer work, choosing organizations that pique her interest or to which she can contribute value. She cochairs the kitchen committee at her church and serves on several boards. For example, she is a trustee of the Japanese American National Museum (JANM). Having studied Japanese in college, traveled with the Experiment in International Living to Japan, and funded educational and cultural initiatives about Arkansas' internment camps while president of the Winthrop Rockefeller Foundation, she saw participation on the JANM board as an obvious vehicle for linking the internment experience to the larger story of democracy in America. "What I care most about is benefiting people, and not just blacks, who are at the margins of our society. It is all about *respect*, which I realized at a young age."

Sybil is writing a memoir entitled *Guest in a Strange House.* The title is meant to convey the notion, particularly to young people, that a black person in America is not a powerless victim, but someone who makes lemonade out of the lemons she has been given and does it with gusto. "It is important to choose your life; do not just let it happen to you!" She will no doubt mention in her memoir that she was inducted into the Arkansas Black Hall of Fame in 2005 and was given the James Joseph Award from the Association for Black Foundation Executives the same year. She will also explain how her parents and grandfather were early role models for her, making it inevitable that she grew up with the idea of working, going out into the world, and accomplishing things. "All black mothers in Little Rock *had to* work. They worked, juggled family responsibilities, and in fortunate cases like my mother, then went to college and had a career."

She plans to continue working "as long as I am of sound mind or until I drop!" Though her energy level gradually diminishes as she ages, Sybil feels it is all right to do somewhat less so long as she keeps contributing to the work that will still remain to be done after she fully retires. "I know I am going to touch the future. What I have invested in will go on much longer than I will," she says with conviction. And that is what keeps the spark glowing.

Gail Collins's narration of women's liberation over the past fifty years details significant developments that accelerated the entry of females into the workforce: birth control and the sexual revolution, a rising divorce rate, greater awareness of civil rights, a demand for more women workers, and the growing popularity of the two-income family.[25] By the 1980s, Collins notes, women were not only making money to help support their families but also having serious careers. Women were attending college in greater numbers and going on to pursue professional training in fields like medicine and law that had previously been off limits. At the millennium, "there were very few fields in which women had not made major inroads."[26] Then the recession clinched it: not only were more women deciding to work through their child-bearing years, "*women were going to work throughout their lives*" (italics added). [27]

I, for one, was a founding member of the National Organization for Women (NOW) affiliate in my town in the late 1960s. I co-led a committee that examined images of women in books, magazines, television, films, and other media. In the era of *Father Knows Best, Ozzie and Harriet,* and *Leave It to Beaver,* print or television ads usually showed moms mopping the kitchen floor, vacuuming, polishing, baking, or extolling the virtues of a refrigerator or washing machine. Pretty young women were portrayed in automobile ads as decorations to attract the eyes of male consumers. In addition to the stereotypical housewife in a frilly apron, women were pictured as helpers of various kinds and seldom as active participants or executives in male-dominated professions.

Forty years later, Helen Mirren and others have played super-tough detective roles and reality TV shows feature athletic young women in survival mode. Reviewer Daphne Merkin observes film studios taking a calculated risk with movies that appeal to middle-aged and older women, for example, Nancy Meyers's hit film, *It's Complicated.*[28] In sharp contrast with a youth-obsessed movie culture, writer-director-producer Meyers presents Meryl Streep as a self-sufficient, energetic, and accomplished older businesswoman "bombarded with reminders of her vanished youthfulness everywhere she turns," and sets her "in an alternate universe, where she is not only visible but desirable just the way she is." Merkin goes on, "In this sense (Meyers) is proposing the somewhat radical notion that there are *second acts* in women's lives (italics added) and that they don't necessarily hinge on being a desperate housewife in search of the next 'It' bag or a cougar on the prowl." Moreover, Meyers has "defied the conventional wisdom that women are *over*—both societally and professionally—past a certain age."

Lest we get carried away by media portrayals of women overcoming obstacles to success, consider former *New York Times* reporter Lisa Belkin's sobering explication of the "new gender gap" in which women are the majority of workers: "some are opting back in, and many others, who never left, are more likely to find and keep their jobs than men. Once again, the reasons for this are not entirely a function of the clout of women but of the predicament of men and less a sign of how far women have come than of how far they have left to go."[29] Bottom line—on average, women (of all ages) in the United States are still paid less than men regardless of education level and occupation: in 2008 women's earnings were 80 percent of men's, according to the US Bureau of Labor Statistics (BLS). Earnings were only slightly better by 2011 when median weekly earnings for women who were full-time wage and salary workers were $683 or 82.4 percent of the $829 median for men. However, black women's median earnings were 84.4 percent of those for white women and the median earnings of Hispanic women were lower still.[30]

In the next profile we will meet a university professor and fellowship and grant award winner who has devoted her career to teaching and writing about race, gender, and women's work. Dr. Sharon Harley's current scholarship focuses on black women's labor history and racial and gender politics. She anticipates a lengthy and productive work life filled with well-earned intellectual and personal rewards.

PROFILE: SHARON HARLEY

Approaching the peak of her academic career, Sharon Harley does not consider herself to be "older." She is a sixty-two-year-old baby boomer who embraces her cohort's image: "I like knowing I belong to a group of educated and vibrant people who do not act as old as their parents and grandparents might have. By our sheer numbers, we will have political clout and be taken seriously. It is a wonderful development!"

Sharon earned her PhD in US history from Howard University in 1981 and soon joined the faculty in the Department of African American Studies at the University of Maryland, College Park. She is currently an associate professor and until recently chaired the department for fourteen years. The dual focus of her research is black women's labor history and racial and gender politics. She teaches a course on black culture in the United States that regularly attracts between 150 and 200 students, and also gives a course on black women in US history and one on race and labor issues associated with the African diaspora.

Winning a coveted National Humanities Center fellowship enabled Sharon to relinquish her department chair responsibilities and go on leave for the academic year 2010–2011 to write a book entitled *Dignity and Damnation: The Nexus of Race, Gender, and Women's Work*. Although she is "totally obsessed" with finishing the book, she was willing to take a short break from a summertime 2011 writer's retreat to be interviewed because she believes that researchers should help one another out and she shares the interviewer's interest in women's work.

Two equally prestigious fellowships that helped advance her scholarly work were spent at the Woodrow Wilson International Center for Scholars and at the W. E. B. Du Bois Institute for African and African American Research at Harvard University. Other recognition took the form of Ford and Rockefeller Foundation grants and the Letitia Woods Brown Memorial Book Prize in 2007 from the Association of Black Women Historians.

The Great Recession hit when Sharon was remarrying and, what with her job security at the university and a good income, its impact has been minimal.

Her second husband is an electrical engineer who, being slightly younger than Sharon, does not plan to retire for perhaps another fifteen years. She also has a twenty-five-year-old daughter who (like a lot of young adults) is living in New York City on a small salary. Mom has been helping her to cover expenses.

Sharon has multiple reasons for staying in the workforce: there are financial incentives—the income allows her to help support her daughter and to boost future Social Security benefits; there are intrinsic rewards—finding satisfaction in work, the feeling that her scholarship and teaching do make a difference. She is approaching the peak of her career in fine shape. "I am in good health and usually feel vigorous, but I have begun to notice that my energy level is lower than when I was in my thirties and forties. Ideas flowed more freely then, too!" she observes.

"Wrestling with this book has caused me to postpone for a year or two thinking about the rest of my career let alone eventual retirement. I know I would not want to give up the academic life and my contacts with fellow academicians, graduate students, and post-docs. Once the book is published I would like to become a full professor and either remain at the university or perhaps work at a small liberal arts college where teaching is highly respected or at a public policy institute. Above all, I do not want to work at my current highly stressful pace more than another five years; after that I can envision another five or ten years, provided that I have a reduced teaching load." Other possibilities for the future revolve around writing biographies of largely overlooked African American women and working internationally, perhaps teaching in Europe on a Fulbright grant or collaborating with colleagues in South Africa and Ghana.

At some point much farther down the road, Sharon expects to attend a retirement seminar and make some firmer plans. Until then she is managing her fiscal, intellectual, and personal resources well. Her biggest problem today is finding time for everything she enjoys outside of work, including participation in a women's writing group and a wonderful book group, Catholic Church activities, reading, travel, and fitness. She prides herself on keeping her figure by playing tennis all year round, walking, and working out four or five times a week. "Thanks to my hair style and clothes and being in decent shape, I look much younger than I really am! A positive work-life balance helps me to manage stress and is really important to me. I don't need antidepressants. I am blessed with spiritual wholeness."

Family, friends, and colleagues are a major part of her life. She talks with her eighty-three-year-old mother and sister every day and with her daughter nearly as often. "Family is the core of my life. My parents taught me to respect and be considerate of other people. I was also influenced by various high school teachers and, later on, by academic colleagues who showed me how to be a productive and active scholar." It seems that Sharon learned her lessons very well.

As Professor Harley could tell us, the variation in earnings associated with race is especially pronounced for the working poor. Irrespective of age, black and Hispanic women are "significantly more likely" than white or Asian women to be counted among the working poor.[31] The following labor force statistics from the Current Population Survey indicate working women between the ages of fifty-five and sixty-four who live below the poverty level as a percentage of the total in the labor force for twenty-seven weeks or more: 2.9 percent white, 4.9 percent black or African American, 4.8 percent Asian, and 7.7 percent Hispanic or Latino. For working women sixty-five years and older who live below the poverty level, the rates are: 2.4 percent white, 4.3 percent black or African American, 0.2 percent Asian, and 3.2 percent Hispanic or Latino. When it comes to gender and poverty status, the percentages of fifty-five to sixty-four-year-old working men and women living below the poverty level are nearly identical (3.3 percent and 3.2 percent respectively); but poor working men in the sixty-five-and-older category are faring somewhat better than women in the same age group (2.0 percent compared to 2.5 percent).[32]

With lower cumulative earnings and relatively fewer years of paying into Social Security, the average woman can look forward to retirement benefits that are less than the average man's. She would have to stay in the workforce to redress the balance. However, if she (a) loses her job and cannot find another one, or (b) finds re-employment at a lower salary than she received in her old job, she will be in a bind when, as is likely, the Social Security retirement age goes up again. She would be contributing less to Social Security (under the lower pay scenario) or nothing at all (under the no-job-at-all scenario), and she would also have to wait longer to be eligible for full retirement benefits.

Long before Nancy Meyers made *It's Complicated*, Maggie Kuhn and her Gray Panthers were fighting for recognition and championing their peers' vitality and effectiveness. Kuhn founded the organization in 1970 when she was forced into retirement at age sixty-five.[33] It was not until sixteen years later (in 1986 and too late for Maggie Kuhn) that a part of the federal Age Discrimination in Employment Act (ADEA) abolished mandatory retirement, but it is not entirely gone. Policies in some sectors of the corporate world, at law firms for instance, mandate retirement when a designated age is reached, and some types of employment terminate early due to physical requirements, such as police work, firefighting, and commercial airplane piloting.

The founders of the Gray Panthers were "lively, quick-witted, controversial, and action-oriented." Gray Panthers claim "old people and women constitute America's biggest untapped and undervalued human energy source."[34] Subsequently, other national organizations dedicated themselves specifically to older women's quality of life issues. Two of these are Older Women's League (OWL) founded in 1980 and Wise Older Women (WOW) founded in 2001.[35] What qualifies a person for membership in this type of organization? That is, when does a woman decide she has become "older"? Chronological age is no longer synonymous with one's stage of life. In the next chapter I will present the many definitions of "older."

3

Beyond Age Discrimination

Connotations of aging and retirement are often ominous. Among titles of recent books in a series on the study of aging are the following words: "crisis," "suicide," "mistreatment," "risk," "struggle," and "uprooted." Only one title in the series mentions "success." This negativity should come as no surprise, since aging has been historically and commonly associated with poverty in Western societies.[1] Still, for fortunate women it has always been possible to enjoy a "good" old age. For example, what constituted a "good" old age for financially secure, independent eighteenth-century older women in Britain and Colonial America involved religious devotion, a network of family and friends, and intellectual pursuits, especially reading.[2] Of course, many variables in addition to financial security, family, friends, and books could determine whether a woman would enjoy a comfortable old age. Then, as now, health, social class, or geographical location could also make a big difference.

Working (outside the home) was not usually part of the equation for the well-off eighteenth-century woman. However, I was intrigued to learn from my husband, a scholar of social welfare in preindustrial England, that the elderly would try to preserve their independence as long as possible. Thus, older women of the gentry could supervise their estates or property; "middling" sorts of businesswomen could engage in the needle trades, victualling (food provisioning), caring work, or retailing; and the marginally poor might be charwomen, hawkers, or nurses. Even if they lost their independence and had to "go on the parish" for assistance, they could also be required to work as caregivers for sick or infirm parishioners.[3]

Fast forward to 1900 when 5.1 million or just over 20 percent of all women in this country worked, again to 2008 when nearly 68 million women worked, even married women and mothers with young children, and again to 2014 when the number of working women is projected to be nearly 76 million, representing all social class and income levels.[4] In the next chapter I will pin down what proportion of the labor force is female and what proportion is older, but first I have to determine what "older" means.

Definitions of "older" vary widely, and when applied to workers, the descriptor has many implications. The ADEA applies to workers forty and above.[5] For the US BLS, the starting point can be sixty-five or it can be fifty-five. Then again, according to other researchers, "old" does not begin until eighty.[6]

To make it even more difficult to pin down the age question, it has almost become a cliché to claim that eighty is the new seventy, seventy is the new sixty, sixty is the new fifty, and so on. Owing to Americans' increased longevity and generally good health, some even go so far as to say today's eighty-year-olds are like sixty in terms of well-being and vigor and sixty-year-olds are like forty-year-olds.[7] What's more, there are different nicknames for the generational cohorts. Boston College's Sloan Center on Aging and Work researchers call those born before 1946 "Traditionalists," followed by the "Baby Boom" (1946–1964), "Generation X" (1965–1980), and "Generation Y" (born since 1980).[8] Others employ slightly different nicknames and demarcations to characterize today's cross-generational workplace: "Veterans" (1922–1943), "Boomers" (1943–1960), "Xers" (1960–1980), and "Nexters" (1980–2000).[9] Or perhaps you prefer "Millennials" (born 1977–1998). No matter how useful such generalizations and categorizations are, let us be careful not to allow them to negate the individuality of older persons and the particular ways in which they manage their affairs.

Varying definitions of "older" can also depend on the career field in which one works. The working life of a surgeon, pilot, or firefighter is abbreviated when a prescribed age is reached; for an older teacher or social worker it is not. A retirement-eligible veteran teacher explains to an *Education Week* writer why she is still on the job and has no intentions of retiring by describing her assets as a teacher leader:

> I have had to go in for spare parts . . . but I think I have still got what it takes to make it in middle school. I teach alongside colleagues who are younger than my own children and some of whom are my former students. . . . They have energy and technology skills that I do not, but I have pedagogical skill and experience that I can share and that they want. I am a trusted sounding board and a source of institutional knowledge to my younger principal. . . . [And here's the clincher] being a certain age allows me the luxury of time, focus, patience, and humility that I did not have at a younger age.[10]

Age is particularly sensitive in the business world where older workers are often stereotyped as less productive and more expensive, particularly during an economic downturn.[11] While older employees may be appreciated for their work ethic, experience, and ability to get along with coworkers, they are also apt to be seen as resistant to change and unable or unwilling to learn new technologies.[12] At a major international investment firm, a young-looking middle-aged friend of mine who is on the fast track agonizes over keeping her real age a secret from her colleagues. At her firm fifty is considered old. A thriving high tech market research company portrayed in a *New York Times* column is said to still value experienced hands. "Experienced" here means baby boomers in their late forties with a few, including the founder/CEO, in their fifties. And it is not unusual for mature workers to (gasp!) report to a much younger supervisor.[13]

One study of older women workers says societal attitudes defining women in their forties as "over the hill" create "virulent combinations of sex and age discrimination for middle-aged women."[14] A boomer of my acquaintance who is approaching age sixty and is too young to participate in my survey nonetheless wanted to share her thoughts with me. She argues that it is not only ludicrous to think older women are over societally, but it is also myopic for employers to jettison their professional talents. Moreover, she says, "Our generation is going to have no choice about continuing to work for longer than we might prefer. I chose a field—engineering project and program management—specifically in the belief that it would be, if not precisely an asset to be an older worker, at least not a liability. However, ageism is definitely out there even in my field and it causes me concern. These stereotypes need to be demolished. For one thing, US businesses cannot afford to prematurely put out to pasture an entire generation of our most educated and experienced professionals. Consider that macro-economic angle!"

Nature provides an intriguing example of productive employment for aging workers. Leaf-cutter ants in the rain forests of Panama use their razor-sharp mandibles to chomp leaves into a foliage used for fungi farming, the main food supply for the ant colony. A University of Oregon research scientist, Robert Schofield, discovered what happens when the mandibles wear down and become dull after all that chomping and the ants can no longer cut leaves. They do not stop working! They simply take on a new and no less essential job function. Instead of being relegated to the "aging ant" shelf (or a worse fate), they take on a new job that contributes to the welfare of the colony, carrying cuttings back to the nest.

Unfortunately, the human domain is not always as enlightened as the ant world. Discrimination against older persons in the workplace can come from any direction—employees or employers, either younger or older. According to psychologists Becca Levy and Mahzarin Banaji, who coined the term "implicit ageism," discrimination against older people is more entrenched than any of the other 'isms'.[15] Despite the existence of ADEA prohibitions against age discrimination since 1967, the American Association of Retired Persons (AARP) finds that negative stereotypes about older workers persist. The ADEA did not prevent Maggie Kuhn, for one, from being forced out. In fact, ADEA has dealt with more cases of termination over the years (particularly on behalf of men and women younger than normal retirement age) than of hiring.[16]

Jo-Ann Hoffman, now sixty-nine and planning to live to be 105, is all too familiar with age stereotyping. She feels the pressure about appearances and beauty articulated by sociologist of aging Laura Hurd-Clarke.[17] She wants to be seen as more than a "declining body," as gerontologist Margaret Cruikshank would put it.[18] So Jo-Ann keeps her hair the same reddish-brown it always was. Even when she was going into the hospital for a hip replacement four years ago, she made sure to have her hair done the day before. "When a woman shows gray hair, she is considered to be old and useless, while a man's gray hair makes him appear distinguished. There is no way I am going to let people look at me and judge my abilities and my work based on the color of my hair!" Jo-Ann also makes sure that her clothing is professional, as that too helps her to be taken seriously. One thing she cannot do anything about: these days she must walk with a cane, owing to nerve damage incurred during the surgery, and some people look at her skeptically when they see the cane. Even though Jo-Ann has suffered job loss because of her age, she is determined to keep working because it means she is still professionally viable—that is, off the shelf and contributing to society.

PROFILE: JO-ANN HOFFMAN

After doctoral work in education years ago, Jo-Ann Hoffman embarked on a long career at Rutgers University's Cooperative Extension Service in the Department of 4-H Youth Development. For thirty-five years she trained adults to become 4-H instructors in clubs, schools, and special education programs. She is particularly proud of the job-preparedness model she developed for working with 4-H youngsters in *urban* settings. The goal was to teach kids about employment by giving them actual business experience. The kids ran fruit and vegetable stands, pricing and selling the produce and sharing in the profits. They were taught to dress, speak, and act appropriately. The model was replicated across the nation. Nevertheless, inevitably there were changes at the university and Jo-Ann decided to step down in 2001 and accept *emeritus* status. What had been her base at Cook College was to become the School of Environmental and Biological Sciences. It was not so much the name change as the expectation that she sit behind a desk and write grants. That was not for her; she was a *doer*.

Retirement lasted for all of two weeks. She cleaned her house from top to bottom, relined the kitchen shelves, and was thoroughly bored. When her well-meaning friends said, "You are retired. You do not have to work," Jo-Ann would answer, "Oh, yes, I do! Getting paid means I am still viable and contributing to society, and I am not on the shelf."

She was in good enough shape to land a job as a physical trainer for a Curves health club and fitness center. She had the early morning shift, starting at 6:30 a.m. After one year, the director decided that all trainers had to be youthful, and sixty-year-old Jo-Ann was out of a job. She tried substitute teaching for a year in the Trenton public schools. Next, for three years she managed the *virtual* office of Contact USA (CUSA), the national organization that coordinates staff training and program accreditation for affiliated local CUSA crisis hotlines. The other shoe dropped when the director eliminated the virtual office in favor of a real office located in another state. Finally, Jo-Ann decided to start Highland House, her own educational consulting business.

Her present job is a continuation of the 4-H work she did for so many years at Rutgers. As a consultant, she works part time under an historic preservation grant as an educational interpreter and membership coordinator for the Howell Living History Farm in Lambertville, New Jersey. Operated by the Mercer County Park Commission, the farm is more than 250 years old. In its present form it is a public park and educational facility where youth and adults participate in hands-on farming activities to learn about farm life in Pleasant Valley, primarily from 1890 to 1910. When Inez Howell made a gift of the farm to Mercer County in 1974 in memory of her husband, she stipulated that it be used as a living history farm where children and 4-H youth groups can try their hand at tree planting, riding a donkey, cleaning out a stable, putting the manure back into the earth, plowing, sowing, canning, and pickling. She added two more pieces of advice, one serious and one whimsical—remember that girls can do these chores, too, and do not forget rainbows and swinging on grapevines!

Jo-Ann chooses to work part time so she does not have to give up other things she enjoys, such as babysitting for her ten-month-old great-niece one day a week. She maintains a good balance between work and leisure. "I kept a calendar when I was at the university. I still have a calendar and it is very full!" For example, she continues to be associated with CUSA as volunteer associate director of Mercer County's twenty-four-hour crisis hotline. She coordinates the internship program that prepares CUSA staff to respond to callers experiencing depression, grief, money problems, or medical woes.

Jo-Ann also serves on the National Committee of OMEP (Organisation Mondiale pour l'Education Préscolaire/World Organization for Early Childhood Education), an international, nongovernmental, and nonprofit organization concerned with all aspects of early childhood education and care. She sings in her church choir and teaches a second grade religious education class. She plans to provide coaching to diocesan lectors (church readers) who need help with their presentation skills, work for which the diocese will pay her a fee. She is active with Soroptimist International, a worldwide organization of some ninety thousand business and professional women who strive to improve the lives of women and girls in their communities. For example, Jo-Ann's local chapter purchased protective vests for Trenton policewomen. (A woman's vest cost twice as much as a man's and many policewomen could not afford it.)

Jo-Ann also has been sponsoring a Ugandan schoolgirl who is now a sophomore in high school. Through the Arlington Academy of Hope founded by a Ugandan couple, Jo-Ann pays for the girl's education, school uniform, school lunch, medical care (malaria is a widespread problem), and a portion of a teacher's salary. She has already been to Uganda to help set up a library in the village school and a medical clinic in a nearby village, and she plans to return again in the dry season. Clearly this is an unusually resourceful and charitable person.

A single woman with no children of her own, Jo-Ann has made friends with people in all age groups. She credits her aunt, who was a single woman with no children, for the sage advice she has followed: build a "chosen" family for yourself. Aunt Rose told Jo-Ann to choose men and women of different ages whom she can help now and who would be able to help her when she needs it. She would say, "If all your friends are the same age as you, chances are most of them will become infirm or will die." Jo-Ann heeded the advice. She is godmother and aunt to several young people whom she can call upon to help with tasks, such as car shopping or setting up a Christmas tree.

Another mentor for Jo-Ann was Helen Huston, an "absolute phenomenon made of velvet-covered steel," who died at 100. Jo-Ann explains, "She was a person of today way back when. She never married. A successful businesswoman with many friends, she founded Soroptimist International of Trenton in 1942. When she was ninety-nine, she was still volunteering for Contact, calling daily to check on homebound people."

These two women were Jo-Ann's role models socially and career-wise. They taught her to give of herself to help others, to look ahead, to always try something new and different, to set up a savings or pension plan, and not wait until too late to figure out what to do after retirement. Most of all, they taught her to remain active and professionally viable so there would be no danger of being put on the shelf.

The higher incidence of ADEA termination cases may occur because discrimination in hiring is hard to detect and even harder to prove. This is true for discrimination on the basis of race as well as age and gender. Data from the US Department of Labor for July through September 2009 showed racial disparities among female job seekers of all ages and qualifications in New York City: 12.1 percent were black, 11.6 percent were Hispanic, and 7.1 percent were white. The gaps were even more pronounced for unemployed men: 20 percent of all male job seekers citywide were black, 12 percent were Hispanic, and 7.6 percent were white.[19] Even a college degree from a prestigious institution is no guarantee of success for a person of color in the job market: in 2009, black women and men with college degrees were twice as likely to be unemployed as their white counterparts (roughly 8 percent vs. 4 percent) across the country.[20]

When an older person submits a job application with resume and cover letter to the human resources department, the oh-so-polite response is apt to be along the lines of the following (e-mail) rejection message: *Thank you for your application to the following position at _____. Although we are unable to further your candidacy for this specific position at this time, we appreciate your interest.* A 2008 survey conducted by the Boston College Center for Retirement Research found that employers believe older workers are too expensive and their skills are outdated; they were also reluctant to train or promote older workers based on the suspicion that they would not stick around for long.[21] Organizations and institutions unfriendly to older workers might as well post a big sign saying, "No older folks need apply," a throwback to nineteenth-century attitudes when companies blatantly announced which groups were unwelcome. How do we reconcile such myopia with the fact that many older persons *are* in the paid workforce today even when unemployment rates are at their highest in years?

Despite wars, earthquakes, droughts, and other natural disasters, the world's population is aging. All around the globe, demographic and socioeconomic trends are associated with unprecedented gains in the average age of the world's population, the National Institute on Aging at the NIH reports.

Longevity among the oldest-old (eighty and up) globally is projected to increase 233 percent between 2008 and 2040 and 160 percent for the population aged sixty-five and over, compared with 33 percent for the total population of all ages.[22] Japan is a leader in regard to longevity with nearly 25 percent of residents over age sixty-five. A priority among the Japanese is "a society where the elderly can live with *ikigai*" or a life worth living, *Boston Globe* deputy editorial page editor Dante Ramos observes.[23] For the many seniors who are healthy, a job enables them to remain active and productive. "Japan's experience shows that, while the aging of society looks mainly like a problem for the social-welfare system when it appears on the horizon, it reveals other dimensions when it arrives."[24] Older residents represent an economic force and a pool of talent, "a mountain of treasures."

It is well known that increases in longevity stem from improved availability of education, nutrition, and health care, among other things. Some facts from Experience Corps bear this out:

> By 2030 the number of Americans fifty-five and older will be 31 percent of the total population compared with 21 percent in 2000.
>
> The number of Americans over sixty-five will more than double, from close to thirty-five million to just over seventy million.
>
> A sixty-five-year-old American female can expect to live another 19.2 years on average (16.3 years on average for males).
>
> The chances of a sixty-five-year-old living to ninety continue to improve.[25]

Our next profile nicely illustrates the Experience Corps points noted previously. In it, Esta Shindler describes her work for the pioneering public health study that has succeeded in identifying and publicizing the risk factors for heart disease and, in so doing, has contributed to the improved health and gains in longevity of so many Americans.

PROFILE: ESTA SHINDLER

Esta Shindler's assertion "I feel young in my heart" is really a double entendre. She is referring to her chronological age (seventy) and, disproving the years, "having a self-image that is younger than I am." However, she could just as well be referring to her long career with the renowned Framingham Heart Study. To know Esta and the job she adores, it is first necessary to understand what the Framingham Heart Study is all about. From the website www.framinghamheartstudy.org we learn:

> In 1948 epidemiologic researchers from the National Heart Institute of the NIH, now called the National Heart Lung and Blood Institute (NHLBI), set out to establish the risk factors for heart disease, the leading cause of death and serious illness in the United States. The institute recruited 5,209 mostly Caucasian men and women between the ages of thirty to sixty-two in Framingham, Massachusetts, who were willing to participate in longitudinal public health research into the common factors or characteristics that contribute to cardiovascular disease (CVD). Researchers began following the development of CVD in the recruits, none of whom had overt symptoms of the disease or had suffered a heart attack or stroke. All participants agreed to give a detailed medical history and undergo close observation and testing every two years, including physical exams and lifestyle interviews that would be analyzed for common patterns. In 1971 a second cohort of 5,124 adult children of the original participants (and their spouses) was recruited, followed in 2002 by the third generation, 4,095 grandchildren of the first cohort. In response to ever-growing diversity in the town of Framingham, the Heart Study added "Omni Cohorts" in 1994 and 2003 composed of participants from various racial and ethnic groups.
>
> Careful monitoring of the Framingham Heart Study population has led to the identification of the major CVD risk factors—high blood pressure, high blood cholesterol, smoking, obesity, diabetes, and physical inactivity—as well as a great deal of valuable information and statistics on the effects of related factors such as blood triglyceride and HDL cholesterol levels, age, gender, and psychosocial issues. This in turn has led to the development of effective treatment and preventive strategies in clinical practice. More recently, with the availability of cell lines on thousands of participants across cohorts, researchers began to study the role of genetic factors in CVD. Other important scientific contributions by the NHLBI and the Framingham investigators involve collaboration with leading researchers from around the country and throughout the world on projects in stroke and dementia, osteoporosis and arthritis, nutrition, diabetes, eye diseases, hearing disorders, lung diseases, and genetic patterns of common diseases.

Esta's job mainly entails doing public relations for the Framingham Heart Study. She is responsible for compiling, editing, and disseminating reports to the NHLBI and to the Observational Studies Monitoring Board that oversees the human subjects research at the Heart Study. She prepares the Heart Study's newsletter and has played a major role in the design, development, and management of the website. She manages the Ethics Advisory Board, composed of participants, clergy, lawyers, physicians and scientists, and community representatives, who advise the Heart Study on ethics issues specifically related to participation in Heart Study research, as well as on the ramifications of genetics research. She supports the work of the Friends of the Framingham Heart Study, and she handles media requests for interviews with participants and research investigators. One of the research scientists she most admires is the Heart Study's brilliant former director, Dr. William Kannel, who hired her twenty years ago. Before his death in 2011 at eighty-eight years of age, he was still coming to work and publishing medical reviews and papers.

When asked to describe the most gratifying aspect of her work, Esta does not hesitate: it is seeing the results of her efforts and receiving the recognition of coworkers and senior investigators at the Heart Study and other research collaborators nationally and internationally. "When I returned after being away on vacation, colleagues made it clear that they were happy that I was back! Apparently, several had been asking where I was." Esta hastens to add, "To be sure, I am not tooting my own horn. It is just that I have been there a long time and it is nice to be appreciated."

Esta points out that in public health *nomenclature* sixty years and older can be classified as "elderly." However, at seventy, although she has gray hair and slightly less energy than she used to have, she certainly does not feel old. And the public health *statistics* regarding increased longevity and quality of life back her up. Obviously, there is a disconnect between conventional public health nomenclature and the abundant evidence that older workers can be productive in many fields.

Although her job can occasionally be frustrating, Esta focuses on the positive. Her philosophy has always been maximizing every day of her life—her relationships, her health—hoping for the best and having a good time. "I love my job and cannot think of a better one. I love the Heart Study and my colleagues are like a second family to me. I could be sitting home and reading and doing needlepoint, which I also love, but there is too much to do! The rewards of working at the Heart Study make it hard to think of leaving," she tells me.

My question about how long she expects to continue working elicits this response from Esta: "It is a Solomonic dilemma. I believe one should always look ahead. I am at a place in my life where I keep wondering whether I should make a change and do something else. Should we move closer to our children and grandchildren in the New York–New Jersey area? Watching our grandchildren grow and interacting with them, seeing the world through their eyes is my greatest joy. Another reason I fantasize about moving there is because it is so interesting and exciting, there is always so much to do. From Gail Sheehy's *Passages* I learned that as we go through one passage we see the next one staring us in the face. We can embrace the next passage or resist it. Embracing usually leads to success. But even though I am quite willing to look ahead, I have not yet figured out the priorities, so I am still going through mental gymnastics to find the right balance."

In fact, Esta admits to being afraid of retiring and "giving up something wonderful" (i.e., her job). "My husband, who is happily retired from his executive recruitment business, has mastered the fine art of relaxation. I have not." The decision about when to retire is entirely up to Esta. Her husband supports everything she wants to do, except moving to New York. He is happy where he is. They have lived in Framingham for forty years and have wonderful friends in the area. Esta can only think of one friend who has not retired. Although she would not mind being free to join in some of their activities, she does not envy her retired friends, only their ability to come and go whenever they wish. She feels she is always juggling everything. "When I get home from work, it seems there is never enough time left to do the things I want and need to do."

Esta describes herself as a person who has always been willing to try things, perhaps a reaction to parents who were overly cautious and discouraged her from taking risks, such as going off to Europe for six weeks with new friends after graduation from Simmons College (she went anyway). She has never been afraid of tackling anything new, including technology. When she met and married her husband, he was an avid downhill skier, so she learned to ski. They and their children became a skiing family, and Esta now considers skiing a passion. She had no trouble with fifty or with sixty, but turning seventy has caught her attention. "Being seventy connotes how short life is. We never know what is around the corner. Twenty years will go by quickly and I will be ninety! I want to be sure that I do what I want to do by then so I have no regrets." She considers her recent birthday to be a milestone, perhaps a signal that she should be giving more thought to next steps. She remains optimistic about the choices.

Mary Catherine Bateson, a well-known explorer of the life cycle, asks us to think of longevity more as a process than as numbers. That is, it entails more than a mere extension of years into true old age. She identifies "a new space part-way through the life course, a second and different kind of adulthood that precedes old age.[26] Bateson says that this stage, Adulthood II, is characterized by "active wisdom" because of its potential for self-reflection and galvanizing one's experience and perspectives over a lifetime into greater engagement, new directions, new insights and choices, and discovering ways of making significant contributions to family and society at large.

Whatever the senior years are called—in addition to Adulthood II popular designations are "Prime Time,"[27] "The Second Half,"[28] or "The Third Chapter"[29]—convention used to place the time for retirement and enjoyment of leisure somewhere between sixty and sixty-five. (As noted previously, Social Security has weighed in by hiking the preferred age for collecting full benefits and may raise it again in the future.) What are talented and experienced men and women to do with themselves in retirement? Here is what two prominent voices recommend.

Marc Freedman says they should not let society shove them off into the sunset. He urges men and women to transform what it means to age by dedicating their "prime time" to civic engagement and volunteering. He advocates balancing personal fulfillment with responsibility to others. Freedman advises the "encore careerist" to "stop climbing the ladder and start making a difference" and to "swap income for impact." Less than two dozen pages later, however, perhaps in acknowledgment of economic hard times and the perils of outliving one's savings, he revises those goals to include continued income *as well as* social impact. In any case, an "encore career" should be productive and meaningful, not mere busy work. By "riding the wave of longevity and health toward a future that works better for all generations," Freedman says, seniors can enter an entirely new phase of individual and social renewal. [30]

In a similar vein, Sara Lawrence-Lightfoot speaks about the need to be needed and a "yearning for lives of active engagement, purposefulness, and new learning." [31] She finds that the men and women she interviewed challenge cultural assumptions about older adults—mental, physical, and spiritual deterioration, lessened capacity for learning, and the benefits of living in retirement communities—all of which underestimate people in their Third Chapter. [32]

Even so, many seniors do decide to shop for a retirement unit when confronting one or more of the following scenarios: (1) they no longer need a large single-family house or apartment and are unwilling or unable to maintain their property; (2) a single individual or a husband or wife needs assistance with the tasks of daily living; or, (3) a spouse or partner dies. Planned retirement communities, variously known as independent living or active adult communities, assisted living or long-term life care communities, have been appearing all across the country, particularly in states with warm climates, to serve seniors and retirees. The different nomenclature indicates whether on-site assistance and medical care are provided. Some are owner-occupied, some offer only rental units. Some are expensive high-end properties with many amenities, such as a pool, fitness center, walking paths, workshop, library, and convenience store, and some keep the cost somewhat more affordable by offering fewer amenities. Normally, a resident pays an entry fee and monthly fees; depending on the plan, there may also be assisted living fees. Many have age restrictions that effectively separate senior citizens from younger people and children, which is actually another form of putting older men and women on the shelf.

Retirement communities often have a resident council, a mechanism intended to aid communication between residents and the management. In reality, however, council members' opinions and recommendations are not taken very seriously unless management thinks they happen to make good business sense. Competition from newer retirement communities in an area—not residents' suggestions—is what often drives investment in upgrades and improvements. Resident council or not, another problem is resident passivity.

When my extremely independent and outspoken eighty-one-year-old mother moved to a very fine and rather large life care community in the Boston area, she was dismayed to find that the majority of the residents seemed to have surrendered control over policies and procedures to management. "They have become sheep!" she would say disdainfully. "They have traded their independence for the promise of security."

New arrivals, especially those who like her were from out of state, often had a hard time finding friends among the "pioneers" who had been the first cohort to move there. (Among the pioneers who had not moved "over the bridge" to the health care center or Alzheimer's unit were many still remarkably vital residents in their nineties, and some were over one hundred.) Mother was an avid reader, so she joined the library committee. She accepted an invitation to join the synchronized swim team. However, standing in a circle in the pool and patting the water with the other ladies did not count as exercise for her. She was a lap swimmer! She spoke up at resident council meetings, wrote for the newsletter, and tried to rally the livelier residents, to no avail. Finally, she persuaded the activities director to offer a series of discussion groups designed to help new residents adjust to communal life, and she volunteered to lead them. As a retired psychotherapist with many years of experience and a doctorate under her belt, Mother was well equipped to do so. In her private view, the so-called discussion groups were really therapy sessions.

An independent living facility is the worksite of Ann Arvedon, a personable seventy-one-year-old with whom I have served on the board of our local library and on the team responsible for our "one book, one community" initiative, Framingham Reads Together. Ann shared her insider knowledge of the retirement community with me. It seems that many residents do choose what Sara Lawrence-Lightfoot describes in *The Third Chapter*; that is, they are willing to trade self-determination for the promise of security and in the process run the risk of succumbing to the passivity that so aggravated my hypercritical mother.

PROFILE: ANN ARVEDON

Ann Arvedon is the concierge for the independent living portion of a suburban retirement community called Emeritus at Farm Pond, which is in my hometown of Framingham, Massachusetts. With few exceptions, the independent living population is comprised of retired eighty- and ninety-year-olds who are still relatively active. Assisted living care is also available at Emeritus should it be needed. There is a *pro forma* resident council.

The eleven-year-old facility is located in south Framingham on the grounds of the former Cushing Hospital, once a complex of ninety-five buildings built to care for thousands of wounded World War II soldiers, which then became a long-term care veteran's hospital and a state-run geriatric facility after the war. The Framingham Peace and 9/11 Memorials and Cushing Chapel are located within the grounds. Farm Pond, on whose shores William Lloyd Garrison and fellow nineteenth-century abolitionists rallied and Chautauqua Society notables performed and lectured to crowds, is just across the street.

Ever modest, Ann does not feel that what she does is as exciting as the work of career women she knows. In her estimation, it is "only a job." Yet this seventy-one-year-old displays enviable dynamism, warmth of personality, and dedication to her job that cannot always be found in younger employees. Typical of Ann are the reasons she cites for continuing to work. "I have to keep busy, and I need to have a place to go when I wake up in the morning! I am happy to have a job I love. It is truly fulfilling work. People look to me to help them and to listen to them. I am easy to get along with, and the residents and families are grateful for a kind word."

Ann is always impeccably coiffed and smartly dressed. "I am the first person people see when they enter the premises, and it is especially important to make a good impression on prospective residents and their family members. Often townspeople who are exercising on the walking paths will stop in to ask questions about the place." People who are thinking about moving from out of state need special attention. Residents who have had to give up driving are often depressed. Ann deals with residents' problems and complaints in person and on the telephone, helps the activity director plan activities and trips, and reminds people of their appointments. "People trust me. I am their go-to person. The day goes by quickly, and I do not have to bring work home."

Ann has worked in this retirement community since the facility was under construction in 1999. At first she and the marketing director worked in a trailer on the premises, then called the Village at Farm Pond. Soon she was asked to bring her marketing skills to bear by covering the front desk and she has been there ever since. While she has won Employee of the Month and

Employee of the Year awards, she does not need that form of recognition to know that she is much appreciated by the residents.

When her two children were of school age, Ann began working part time. She started out in marketing by developing health management plans for Blue Cross, arranging community relations events, and acting as an ambassador for health plans at shopping malls and finally moving to the Caring for Children Foundation where she was responsible for enrolling low-income children in state health insurance and dental plans. Eleven years ago, a Framingham friend gave her a tip about job possibilities at a soon-to-be built Village at Farm Pond retirement property in town, and she was hired.

Keeping busy is Ann's primary reason for continuing to work. However, she readily admits to being worried whether she will have enough to live on in the future. When her husband, Stuart, admonishes her to spend less—he has done so for all of their forty-seven years together—Ann retorts that it gives her pleasure to indulge the grandchildren.

Stuart is eleven years older than Ann, a semi-retired electrical supply distributor who works "at his own pace." He does not mind Ann's working thirty-two hours a week but would like her to cut back on some of her other activities and be home more often. He himself prefers to be less active these days, and it does concern her that they are out of sync energy-wise.

Ann definitely has plenty to do. "I always manage to get in what I want to do, especially babysitting for my grandchildren after work and playing mahjongg," she grins. Her volunteer work focuses on the local library where she served on the board of trustees for nearly a decade. She helps to run bake sales for the Literacy Unlimited Program at the library and is a founding member of the library committee for Framingham Reads Together. This is the "one book, one community" initiative that brought Greg Mortenson, coauthor of the best seller *Three Cups of Tea*, to town in 2009 and celebrated the sesquicentennial of the Civil War: On the Battlefield and the Home Front in 2011. One of her favorite activities is serving on the Community Development Block Grant Committee that gives money to worthy local organizations. Oh, and she was president of the League of Women Voters in its heyday in the 1970s, and she spent sixteen years as an elected member of the Board of Health. What more could she have fit in? "I would have liked to get a certificate in gerontology at UMass/Boston, but now I think it is too late."

Ann and her husband are grateful to be in good health. She plays some golf in the summer because she really enjoys the walking. During the winter, she goes to a personal trainer once a week to work on her balance. Retirement is nowhere in sight. "Age is not a factor in my decision to keep working. And I am not afraid to retire. If I did, I know I would have plenty to do. I would go to lectures and take classes at a university. The real reason is that I simply do not feel old and I love what I do. Am I productive at work? I would say 'over and above.'" In sum, Ann seems to be doing quite well when it comes to balancing.

Although advice to seniors about venturing forth in new directions is very well intentioned, there are very good reasons for delaying retirement, including paying more into Social Security and collecting higher benefits, provided of course that one wants to and is able to keep working. Under the Senior Citizens Freedom to Work Act of 2000, the Social Security outside earnings limit was repealed: recipients who have attained full retirement age no longer have their Social Security benefits reduced if they earn more than a modest income while collecting. Indeed, with this strong incentive, among others, for remaining in the labor force, "the tide may be turning for older workers."[33] Compared to earlier generations, their chances of living a long and healthy life are superior, thus enabling them to postpone retirement and avoid being shoved off into the sunset or put on the shelf altogether. A 2010 MetLife report on employee benefit trends provides corroboration: nearly 60 percent of employees responding to MetLife's national survey said that they expect to work past age sixty-five, a gain of six percentage points over the previous year, and among younger boomers who plan to work past age sixty-five the change from the previous year was even greater.[34]

Researchers Jacquelyn James and colleagues in the Sloan Center on Aging and Work at Boston College make an important distinction: "Some continue to work because they enjoy it and need the meaning, structure and life purpose that work provides, i.e., because *they want to*. Others continue work in order to maintain costly health benefits and/or to supplement inadequate pensions. Some, of course, work because they can ill afford retirement at all: *they have to*" (italics added).[35]

Let us remember that "need" is relative; it can have different meaning for different people. For example, fewer Hispanics and blacks have income from Social Security, earnings, pensions, and retirement savings, compared to whites.[36] And Hispanics are far more likely than whites or African Americans to cite responsibility for the support of family members as a reason for working.[37]

In chapter 4, we will examine the economic climate confronting older workers in the United States and influencing their decision to participate longer in the labor market.

The Employment Situation for Adult Workers in the United States

The magnitude of these dramatic age twists in the employment rates of US workers is historically unprecedented. At no time since the end of World War II did the labor market ever experience such a phenomenon especially between the youngest and oldest workers.—Andrew Sum, Joseph McLaughlin, Sheila Palma, Jacqui Motroni, and Ishwar Khatiwada, Northeastern University Center for Labor Market Studies

At the risk of triggering recession fatigue, we will start with the bad news. Unemployment is protracted; it is not a bubble. The employment situation nationwide as reported by the US BLS[1] gives little cause for optimism. Employers initiated a record number of job layoffs in October–December 2009. Nine major industry sectors had a record high number of mass layoffs for a third quarter. Home foreclosures and bank closures continued apace. The nationwide unemployment rate (for all age groups combined) hit 10.2 percent in October 2009, the highest rate since April 1983, and this figure did not include "marginally attached" workers who sought work unsuccessfully within the past twelve months and "discouraged" jobless individuals who were no longer looking for work.

However, in November and again in December the rate had improved somewhat to 10 percent nationwide. By January and February 2010 it was slightly better at 9.7 percent and hovered there in March. The number of unemployed men and women had dropped somewhat to 14.9 million in

February from 15.7 million four months earlier, but in March it crept up again to 15 million. Among the major worker groups the unemployment rates (not seasonally adjusted) were: adult men 10 percent, adult women 8 percent, whites 8.8 percent, blacks 16.5 percent, Hispanics 12.6 percent, and Asians 7.5 percent.

The largest job losses were in male-dominated fields such as construction, manufacturing, and retail trade. In March 2010, construction was still hurting, as well as the information industry, transportation, and warehousing. In contrast, health care employment continued to be very, um, healthy. Owing largely to differences across industries, at 10.5 percent the jobless rate for men of all ages surpassed the rate for women at 8.6 percent.[2]

Also in March, 44.1 percent of the unemployed, or over 6.5 million individuals, had been out of a job *long term* (twenty-seven weeks and over) compared with 35.6 percent the previous October. The number of "involuntary" part-time workers (persons working part time because their hours had been cut back or because they were unable to find a full-time job) was 9.1 million in March. Employers reluctant to take on permanent workers were increasingly turning to temporary help services. As *New York Times* national economics reporter Motoko Rich observes, it seems temporary employees may become an even larger and more entrenched segment of the workforce since employers looking to the bottom line can hire and fire them more easily and often can avoid paying health and retirement benefits.[3] Inevitably, a considerable number of the short-term hires find themselves overqualified for their new jobs and earning lower pay.

And, as discussed in chapter 1, the Pew Economic Policy Group's study of unemployment lasting for a year or more finds joblessness in nearly every industry and occupation and among men and women of all ages and backgrounds. In a curious twist, there are fewer people fifty-five and older in the ranks of the unemployed; yet when workers in this age group do lose their jobs, more than any other jobseekers, they are more apt to remain jobless for a year or longer. The Sloan Center on Aging and Work at Boston College calls older jobseekers struggling to find work during the recession "the new unemployables."[4]

Having examined the overall employment picture, now let's look at the prospects for older men and women in particular. A 2010 AARP snapshot of current population and labor statistics on older workers (older is defined as fifty-five and over) concludes that the picture is "gloomy."[5] A fair share of the employment decline as of September can be explained by temporary US Census jobs ending that month and fiscally struggling local municipalities cutting staff positions. AARP reports that the number of unemployed older workers and their unemployment rate have increased faster since the start of the recession than has been true for younger workers. At 7.2 percent in September 2010, older workers' unemployment rate exceeded the previous all-time high dating back to 1950. In addition, unemployed older jobseekers are staying out of work for a longer time—the average in September was forty-two weeks, compared with approximately twenty weeks at the start of the recession. More than half of them can be categorized as "long-term" unemployed. Other trends experienced by older workers facing sobering economic realities, as reported by AARP include: taking part-time work when full-time work is not available, holding more than one job, choosing self-employment, and becoming discouraged and no longer looking for work.

To put a face to these trends, I interviewed underemployed museum administrator Merrily Glosband. For more than a year following an unexpected layoff from a job she loved, she has been taking part-time and consulting positions and continuing to do volunteer work while conducting an energetic job search. She is by no means discouraged, however. As far as she is concerned, she is merely in transition and her motor is still running.

PROFILE: MERRILY GLOSBAND

Merrily Glosband goes by the nickname Merry. The name is distinctive and it is apt, for she describes herself as a cheerful person. This personality trait comes in handy when you have been unceremoniously let go from a job you held for ten years and loved.

Merry and her husband, an attorney, have three children. In 1983 she began volunteering as a docent at the Peabody Essex Museum (PEM) in Salem, Massachusetts. Years passed, the three children were in high school and college, and in 1992 she began studying for a master's degree in museum administration at Framingham State College all while continuing to volunteer at the museum in a new capacity as a research assistant. By 1996 she had completed her master's and was serving as the (still unpaid) liaison between the PEM staff and a three-man team representing PEM's senior leadership that was working on an expansion of the museum. One member of the triumvirate offered her a choice of three interesting new projects, and in 2000 she was finally on salary in a position that grew to become assistant director of the Education through Cultural and Historical Organizations (ECHO) Project, an educational and cultural enrichment initiative serving hundreds of thousands of children and adult learners in Massachusetts and the United States with a special focus on educational exchange related to Native American art and culture. The ECHO collaborative is funded by the US Department of Education under the No Child Left Behind Act.

For the next ten years, under the auspices of ECHO, Merry worked with Native peoples and Native collections in museums and other cultural institutions belonging to the partnership—the PEM and the New Bedford Whaling Museum in Massachusetts; the *Iñupiat* Heritage Center in Barrow, Alaska and the Alaska Native Heritage Center in Anchorage; the Bishop Museum in Honolulu, Hawaii; and the Mississippi Band of Choctaw Indians in Mississippi. She managed ECHO's many cross-cultural outreach components, such as a performing arts festival that traveled around the country, and oversaw for PEM— along with colleagues at the other collaborating institutions— production of a symphony, a book, and an educational website (ECHOspace .org) for elementary, secondary, and college students and educators. She had just completed the initial arrangements for a national poetry-writing contest when, without warning, she and sixteen other PEM employees were told that they were being let go. She was lucky to be given six months to wrap up loose ends. A year has passed and the museum has not filled her position.

When her job at the museum ended, her ECHO colleagues—the project heads and staff from around the country—threw her a good-bye party during a conference in Washington, D.C. "They paid me such beautiful compliments and presented me with unbelievable gifts. The Hawaiians gave me a feather *kahili* on a bluestone base. Colleagues from Alaska gave me a bentwood and copper carved box filled with heartwarming personal notes, and the folks from Mississippi honored me with a poem, an owl carving, and many good wishes."

Merry made it clear to me that she has definitely not retired. "I am between jobs. I say I am in transition." Her business cards say that she is a Consultant to Museums and Non-Profits. Under her e-mail signature is a quote from

Vincent van Gogh: "What would life be if we had no courage to attempt any-thing?" When I asked Merry what this quote signifies to her, she told me that it is sort of a dig at those who may think she is done working: "Don't put me out to pasture yet. I still want to be involved." A good deal of her time these days is devoted to her job search—she is applying for part-time and full-time jobs that would tap her leadership and management experience—but unfor-tunately, jobs in her field are quite scarce.

Meanwhile, she has been teaching a continuing education course on Mu-seum Exhibitions, How They Work and Why as an adjunct at Salem State College's Institute for Learning in Retirement (Explorers Program). She still volunteers at the PEM as a docent and tour guide because, as she explains, she is not one to hold a grudge just because she was laid off. "The good thing is that now I can go at a more relaxed pace for a while. I had been working so many hours for ECHO, and I did not realize how stressed out I was. I would go to sleep writing notes to myself on the bedside table and would wake up writing more notes."

Merry recently signed an agreement to teach in the Graduate and Profes-sional Studies master's program at Brandeis University beginning in the fall of 2011. She will teach two courses, one on Leadership, Team Building, and Decision Making, which she will teach online (distance learning), and the other on Professional Communications, which she will teach "on the ground" (that is, in person) and online. In preparation for the fall, she is observing one course this semester and the instructor is mentoring her. "I really appreciate the nurturing that I am getting from Brandeis, and I am impressed that the faculty is so welcoming." Actually, the online courses present no problems for her, as she had to learn the latest in technologies when she was studying for her master's degree. "When my old computer died last week, I was able to assemble the new one by myself. I have joined the Facebook and LinkedIn networks, too," Merry asserts confidently.

During this transitional year, she has also been attending workshops for persons receiving unemployment assistance, such as Get Your Motor Run-ning! The workshop must have gotten a lot of participants' motors running, since Merry has continued to meet once a week for coffee at Panera Bread with people she met there. "They are interesting people of all different ages and from all walks of life, and we bonded." The workshop stimulated a variety of other jobseeking activities. For example, Merry has enrolled in a training course, Appreciative Inquiry, to improve her skills as a facilitator. She joined the Boston Facilitators Round Table, which focuses on helping for-profit and nonprofit clients navigate change. She also signed up for the Swampscott chapter of BIG (which stands for "Believe, Inspire, Grow"), an organization for women who are re-inventing themselves. "For $175 per year, I can attend monthly lectures with highly accomplished women who have had amazing careers and are now at home with their kids and looking for the next thing. Of course, my kids are grown and I am the oldest in the group."

At sixty-four, this baby boomer at the leading edge of her age cohort still has a tremendous amount of energy. She goes downhill skiing, walks for three hours straight three times a week, does yoga and Pilates, and works out on an exercise bike. (A PEM colleague once observed that the world would have no energy crisis if Merry's energy could be harnessed.) She finds the time to participate on several boards, heading the New England chapter of Art Table, an organization for mid-level and senior-level women career professionals in the arts; holding a board position in the Massachusetts chapter of the National Museum of Women in the Arts in Washington, D.C.; and serving on the boards of the Boston Artists Ensemble, a chamber music group, and the University of Massachusetts/Amherst Foundation.

Merry is one of three girls raised by a mother who was "pretty independent and self-assertive," according to Merry. She took care of the twins, Margie and Merry, and another daughter, but did not work outside the home. "Our mother's life was devoted to running errands, yet she was a great influence on us. She liked simplicity and had a flair for design. We had a few art lessons. Margie, who became a terrific art teacher, was the one with true artistic talent, an innate ability to express herself through painting and ceramics. I became someone who could always be counted on to be effective and efficient. I was especially good at building relationships with all different kinds of people, just what my work with Native Americans in the ECHO Project has required."

Twins Merry and Margie recently did some research into the exact time of their birth and learned that there was a five-hour discrepancy between the time their mother remembered and the actual recorded time. With the new information in hand, Merry had an astrologer chart her and her sister. It turns out that the twins were not born under Jupiter after all; they were born under

Venus, who represents art and beauty. "How appropriate for the two of us, considering the careers we chose without ever knowing it was Venus!" Merry exclaims with a laugh. "Now I hope that the positive effects of the planetary alignment will carry over to my job prospecting."

On account of the dismal employment picture nationwide, the demand for services at public libraries is skyrocketing. Record numbers of men and women arrive at libraries day and night to use the computers for job searching, resume writing, and online applications. Print resources tell readers how to bounce back after a layoff and get to work on finding a job. Laid off men and women are supposed to rise above it and get back on the career track (or, as Merry was advised at the Department of Unemployment Assistance workshop she attended, "Get your motor running!"). There are guides to interviewing, building a resume, writing a cover letter, and finding a job. Cheery book titles aim their pitches to the over-forty jobseeker, evidently considered to be an older worker by some authors. Ex-offenders can find advice tailored to their particular circumstances. With numerous career employment websites, computer and resume help is usually available from library staff. Similarly, the services of state and local career centers are in greater demand than ever as unemployed men and women ask for job search and application assistance and education and training opportunities.

Now for the good news about older people in the workplace. Fortunately, by some measures there is a considerable amount of good news. As Henry Wadsworth Longfellow wrote, age can mean opportunity though it takes a different guise and may not be discerned immediately. Counterintuitively, the presence of older adults in the workplace has been increasing for about ten years. At the same time that unemployment of older workers continues to rise, many other seniors (like the women in my study) have been successful in holding on to their jobs or landing new ones. As reported by AARP economic policy researcher Sara Rix, US BLS data show that labor force participation has actually grown for men and women sixty-five and older since the recession began: the number of labor force participants (both employed and unemployed-but-looking-for-work) in that age category increased and their participation rate went from 16.3 percent in December 2007 to 17.7 percent in September 2010.[6] When only the employed in that age group are counted, there were 3,439,000 men and 2,830,000 women for a total of 6,269,000 workers in 2010, a 3 percent increase over the total for the previous year.[7]

While it is obvious that men continue to outnumber women overall in the labor market, it is quite surprising that the fastest-growing cohort *by rate of increase* in the paid workforce is women sixty-five and older.[8] How can it be? What is the context for this phenomenon? There are both quantitative and qualitative explanations. If statistics make your eyes glaze over, feel free to skip directly to the qualitative discussions in the following chapters where the specifics regarding older professional women and their reasons for choosing paid employment over retirement are examined. Here we have the quantitative picture, broken down by age and gender.

We will start by considering participation in the labor market from an *age* standpoint: there are simply more older Americans than ever before, period. By 2018, the fifty-five-and-older civilian noninstitutional cohort is expected to total 91.6 million Americans, an increase of 21 million over the previous ten years.[9] The sixty-five and older population is outpacing that of the total population as well as the population under sixty-five, reports the US Census Bureau. "The older population is on the threshold of a boom" caused primarily by the generation whose forward ranks turned sixty-five in 2011. [10] The bureau projects a total population increase of 18 percent between 2010 and 2030 and a 78 percent gain for the sixty-five and older population. Presently about one in eight Americans is sixty-five or older; in twenty years the ratio will be close to one in five.[11]

More of these older Americans are participating in the workforce. US BLS data show that the total labor force is projected to increase by 8.5 percent during 2006–2016, but it is *older workers, not younger, who will account for most of the growth.* The proportion of workers fifty-five to sixty-four is expected to climb by 36.5 percent. But the most dramatic growth is projected for the two oldest groups. The number of workers between sixty-five and seventy-four and those seventy-five and up are predicted to soar by more than 80 percent. By 2016, workers sixty-five and over are expected to account for 6.1 percent of the total labor force, up sharply from their 2006 share of 3.6 percent.[12] By 2018, the fifty-five-and-older cohort will comprise nearly one-quarter of the labor force.[13] According to the Northeastern University Center for Labor

Market Studies, "The magnitude of these dramatic age twists in the employment rates of U.S. workers is historically unprecedented."[14]

With participation rates for the young (i.e., sixteen to twenty-four) and prime (i.e., twenty-five to fifty-four) age groups declining, the US BLS says the fifty-five-and-older age group remains the only group exhibiting significant increases in labor force participation rates now and for the foreseeable future and offers seven reasons for that distinction:

1. Longer and healthier life spans enable additional years of earned income.
2. Availability of employer-based health insurance keeps people in the labor force.
3. Hikes in eligibility for collecting Social Security benefits encourage delayed retirement and reward older workers for each additional year of employment.
4. A shift from defined benefit to defined contribution pension plans, that is, from employer "pay out" to employee "pay in," means benefits accrue with additional years of work.
5. Elimination of most mandatory retirement ages under ADEA.
6. Higher labor market participation rates among better educated citizens.
7. Negative consequences of the current financial crisis inducing older workers, like other groups, to try to remain in the labor market.[15]

Even more remarkable than the increase of older workers overall is the rate of increase among older *women* workers. Here is the quantitative explanation from a *gender* standpoint: as is well known, there are more older women than older men. While Americans in general are experiencing greater longevity and better health overall, life expectancy for females continues to surpass that for males. Older females are already approaching the one-in-five ratio. With respect to labor force participation by gender, since 1950 the rate for older men has declined while the rate for older women has climbed steadily higher.[16] Younger women and prime age women are decreasing their participation while older women in all subgroups are significantly increasing theirs.[17] For women sixty-five and older, the rate increased from 7.3 percent in 1985 to 13.3 percent in 2008.[18]

Looking ten years beyond that, the projected increase in working women who are sixty-five or older between 2008 and 2018 (89.8 percent, or 2,030,000

women) will be greater than any other age group. The second highest projected increase (61.4 percent, or 336,000), though smallest in actual numbers,
is for working women seventy-five years and older.[19]

Mitra Toossi, writing in the US BLS' *Monthly Labor Review Online*, es-
timates labor force participation rates for selected age groups of men and
women in 2018.[20] The projected percentage point increases for women in
both the fifty-five-and-older and sixty-five-and-older categories (5.6 percent
for each age category) are greater than the increases for men in those same
age groups (2 percent and 5.2 percent respectively), while the increase for
men seventy-five and older (3.5 percent) is projected to be one percentage
point higher than for women in that age group (2.5 percent). The BLS expects
the overall trend in favor of higher labor force participation rates for older
women over older men to continue, at least in the near future.

Looking at women's labor force participation from another angle, let us
recall the breakthrough reported in chapter 2: women (in all age groups) now
comprise a majority across American workplaces for the very first time. Moreover, we know that the economic decline has hurt both men and women, but
men have been losing jobs faster than women since the "HE-cession" officially
began in December 2007.

While it is useful to consider gender and age separately, the size and composition of the labor force naturally depend on both factors. Thus, the US BLS
can report that the median age of the women's labor force (41.4 years) inched
past the men's in 2008 and the trend is expected to continue for upward of a
decade owing to the higher level of participation of older women versus men's
pattern of withdrawal from the labor force.[21]

Additional BLS Current Population Survey 2008 *rate-of-increase* data in
figure 1 illustrate striking changes for male and female workers sixty-five
and older. Between 1977 and 2007, employment of male and female workers
sixty-five and over had increased 101 percent, compared to an increase of 59
percent for total employment (sixteen and over). The number of employed
men sixty-five and over rose 75 percent, but employment of women sixty-five
and older had climbed 147 percent. Employed people seventy-five and over,
though only 0.8 percent of the employed in 2007, nonetheless had the most
dramatic gain, increasing 172 percent between 1977 and 2007.[22]

As the BLS explains, the rate increases shown in figure 1 cannot merely be
explained by the aging of the baby boom population because in 2007 the gen-

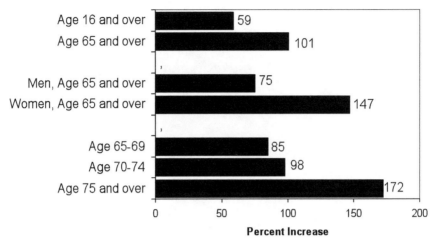

FIGURE 1
Percent increase in employment by age and sex, 1977–2007.
Source: US Bureau of Labor Statistics Current Population Survey.

eration born between 1946 and 1964 had not yet reached sixty-five. Simply, a larger share of people sixty-five and older is staying in or returning to the labor force (those working or looking for work). That the labor force partici-pation rate for older workers has been rising since the late 1990s is especially notable, says the BLS, because the sixty-five-and-over labor force participa-tion rate was at historic lows during the 1980s and early 1990s. See Current Population Survey data in figure 2 for illustration.

Before we examine reasons for the participation turnaround, particularly the share belonging to older professional women, let's look at cross-sector information about employment preferences and some of the salient charac-teristics of the cohort, such as part-time versus full-time status, educational achievement, earnings, and access to retirement benefits.

At approximately the same time participation of older workers began to surge, another turnaround occurred in older worker's employment status—a shift to full-time work. For a while in the early 1990s, according to the BLS, part-time work among older workers was favored over full-time employment. Current Population Survey data indicate that between 1995 and 2007 the trend reversed as the number of older workers on full-time work schedules accelerated and the number working part time declined sharply. In 2007, full-timers accounted for a majority among older workers overall: 56 percent,

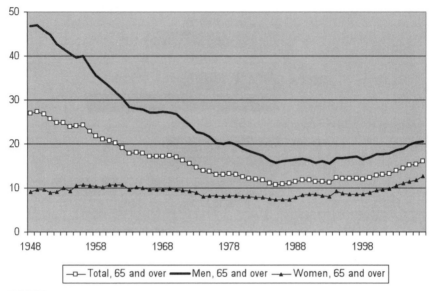

FIGURE 2
Labor force participation rate of workers 65 and over, 1948–2007.
Source: US Bureau of Labor Statistics Current Population Survey.

up from 44 percent in 1995. However, in the throes of the recession and its aftermath, with employers cutting back hours and, in the process, benefits, and turning to temporary help services, the pendulum appears to be swinging back to part-time work, albeit involuntary.

Educational attainment has long been associated with entry into the professions, longer careers, later retirement, and earning levels that can mean higher life expectancy. Current Population Survey data in figure 3 reflect greater educational achievement for men and women sixty-five and older during a recent ten-year period studied by the BLS. There was nearly a six-point jump in bachelor's degrees or more advanced education. More workers had earned a high school diploma or some college credits. And, as we shall see next, these educational gains, plus movement into higher-paying occupations, have over time translated into higher earnings for women.

The peak earning years for women and men are typically between forty-five and sixty-four, and earnings of workers sixty-five and older have tended to be lower. However, recent federal data show earnings of older workers of both genders rising at a slightly quicker rate than wages and salaries of the

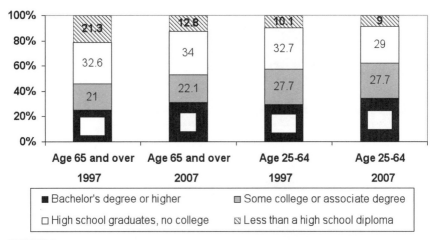

FIGURE 3
Older workers' educational achievement, 1997 and 2007.
Source: US Bureau of Labor Statistics Current Population Survey.

total workforce. Figure 4 reveals that median earnings of older full-time employees in 1979 were 83 percent of those sixteen and up; by 2007 they were at 87 percent.

As noted in chapter 2, historically women's earnings have not been on a par with men's in this country regardless of education level and occupation. In 2011, median weekly earnings for women of all ages who were full-time wage and salary workers were $683 or 82.4 percent of the $829 median for men. While the gap has very gradually narrowed as more women have been able to move into the better-paid professions, the earnings of full-time female workers *sixty-five and older* continue to lag. Current Population Survey data in figure 4 depict the earnings gap of full-time older male and female workers holding steady at 78 percent from 1979 to 2007. However, according to more recent BLS data, the gap grew in 2008: female workers *sixty-five and older* were receiving just 75 percent of their male counterparts' earnings when median weekly earnings of female full-time workers *of all ages* had climbed to a record-high 80 percent of males' earnings.[23]

The recession is not the only state of affairs putting a dent in workers' and retirees' income. Access to retirement benefits is a major factor in decisions about staying in or leaving the workforce. Access hinges not only on employment status (part-timers seldom get any benefits) but also on company policy.

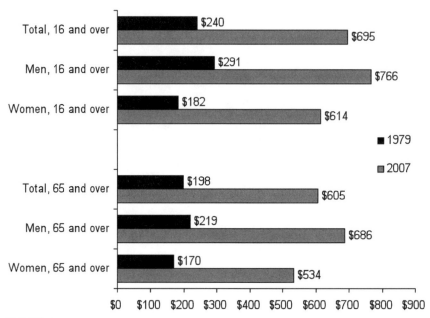

FIGURE 4
Older workers' earnings, 1979–2007.
Source: US Bureau of Labor Statistics Current Population Survey.

The US BLS reports that fewer workers can count on defined benefit plans in which companies pledge to pay workers a specified amount in retirement benefits. As mentioned earlier, traditional "pay out" plans are being replaced by defined contribution or "pay in" plans in which companies contribute a specified amount, but the final payout is not guaranteed. As the BLS explains it, steady retirement income from a pension is no longer assured for many workers, as risk has been transferred from the employer to the eventual retiree. Overall, fewer older women receive pension income than men do and if women do get pension benefits, the median pension is slightly more than half of what men receive.[24]

Retirement benefits and the decisions that hinge on them have been a major part of Clarissa Weiss's job with the City University of New York's (CUNY) labor union for more than three decades. Each and every employee has a story; their needs and timing must be carefully considered. And now she is looking at her own situation. Her husband's recent decision to retire and a growing to-do list of volunteer activities have got her thinking about stepping down from a long and highly rewarding career. However, she will continue working until a qualified replacement can be found and trained, and given the complexities of the job that could take quite a while.

PROFILE: CLARISSA WEISS

Clarissa Weiss has been director of the Pension and Welfare Fund for the City University of New York Professional Staff Congress, a labor union representing the faculty and staff, for thirty-two years. She counsels and educates CUNY faculty and staff about their health benefits, sick leave, sabbaticals, retirement benefits, and so on. She visits all twenty-three of the CUNY campuses for group meetings as well as meeting one-on-one with individual employees to explain their rights under the union contract. In the process she hears all sorts of stories, often very touching. She holds clients' hands and listens. "I have a reputation for being a good listener and a straight shooter. I am not tooting my own horn by saying that. Those qualities happen to be essential for anyone in this line of work." Clarissa also meets with the campus personnel directors and advises the union leadership regarding changes needed in the contract.

She is presently managing implementation of an early retirement incentive program for which there is "unbelievable" demand. Faculty and staff are anxious to take advantage of the incentive and are applying in droves. The last time an early retirement incentive program was offered was 2002. At that time, when a faculty or staff member took early retirement, it meant deletion of a line item in the budget. What is different this time around is that the state agreed to a two-for-one arrangement—for every two individuals who leave, a budget line remains open. As a result, the incentive program is "hot."

When I spoke with Clarissa some months after receiving her survey, she was planning to go part time. She has agreed to stay on until the early retirement incentive program ends and to train her replacement. "Let's face it. I am the institutional memory." Given the intricacies of the job, it should come as no surprise that the union has been unable to find someone to replace her as yet. "Trying to find the next director has been torture!" she exclaims. "It could take six more months and then I will have to train the new person."

Clarissa says she "is lusting" for retirement now. "There IS life after CUNY!" She is looking forward to taking classes (so long as there are no exams). She will do volunteer work in the local Holocaust Center and will continue serving on the board of her synagogue and chairing the Social Action Committee there. "It is our community and it is such an important part of our lives." With their retirement savings, pensions, and health insurance, she and her husband are financially secure despite the recession. Fortunately, their two sons are in good shape employment-wise. "In recent years I have been working more for the joy of it than for the money." She and her husband had been discussing when in the future they might take retirement when her husband, a newspaper editor for more than forty years, was offered a buy-out that was simply too good to pass up. That decision accelerated her thinking about her own retirement. "Believe it or not, I have been working for fifty years, since the age of fourteen. I went to school at night and worked during the day. I think it is time now to move on to a new phase."

Clarissa is a CUNY person through and through; she graduated from Queens College/CUNY where she was a student activist and has been at CUNY almost ever since. During college while going to school at night she was first hired as a community organizer for the Queens District Attorney's Office. Shortly thereafter, she went to work at CUNY as a lobbyist, advocating on behalf of student issues like better access to financial aid, and then moved to Washington, D.C., to pursue the same line of work. Once back at CUNY she continued lobbying, then stepped into the role of director of Pensions and Welfare.

Clarissa describes the labor union as an easygoing place to work. There is great camaraderie among the staff; everyone is very nice to everyone else. Clarissa keeps a bowl of chocolates on her desk and attracts a lot of drop-ins. However, there is also a discernable divide between the union veterans who were hired long ago and the newer staff. "The older women go out to lunch together. The young ones are all vegans! What we talk about differs, too. They go to rallies. We do not. They go out drinking after work. They invite us, but we seldom go. We talk about grandchildren and cluck a lot about their clothes and what they eat. They are like our children. We are admittedly very opinionated about them. We have noticed that people our age have a different work ethic. When I am at work, I *work*. I am not into social media or games, and I read 'real' newspapers, not online apps."

Clarissa has also detected a big difference between older working men and women in the CUNY system who are facing retirement decisions. She thinks a man has a harder time letting go of his professional title than a woman does because a woman identifies less with it. Women are more likely to define themselves in terms of family and community. Still, most professional men and women highly value the collegiality and intellectual stimulation of campus life, perhaps even more than the salary, and are reluctant to leave the college or university for that reason. "I find this is especially true of a woman who started her academic career later, often after having a family. She became a professor at age fifty-one, say, and now she is seventy-one and not ready to retire after only twenty years." Clarissa continues, "In comparison, an older woman who started her career when she was young is probably ready to take the early retirement incentive. If the husband has been retired for several years, and if he is not well, he will urge the wife to take the incentive and retire. He will cry, and she will cry. It can be heartrending to watch them. I often have to ask the husband to step out of the room for a minute to give the wife a chance to tell me what she really wants to do. I have to do that because she is my client. No matter how torn between work and family, she usually decides to do as he asks, and I can understand that."

Clarissa's empathy derives in no small part from having an aging parent. Her mother, Rose, is still a major presence in the family. At eighty-seven she lives independently near her daughter and son-in-law. Although she admits to needing Clarissa's help, she refuses to move into an assisted-living facility. She has never been dependent since leaving Romania as a teenager to find work. She came from a tiny town where only boys could go to school. Rose loved learning and was very bright, so her mother allowed her to sit outside the schoolhouse window to listen and learn. She became a hat maker, the occupation she pursued before her marriage. She came to America as a Holocaust survivor in 1948 with her husband and a young Clarissa. During this time, she took classes in English, teaching her husband and daughter English. Soon she had two children to care for. After her younger child entered junior high school, she went to work for Bloomingdale's. Rose's perseverance (some call it stubbornness) is legendary in the family. And no doubt the drive and accomplishments of her daughter Clarissa will be legendary in the family as well.

As pointed out earlier in this chapter, the US BLS foresees an ever-growing role for older workers in the labor force in the immediate future: for 2006–

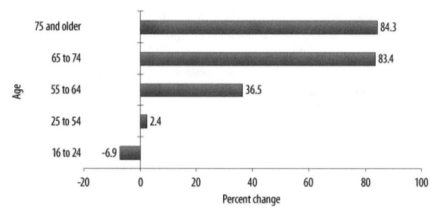

FIGURE 5
Rate of increase in labor force participation by age, 2006–2016.
Source: US Bureau of Labor Statistics Employment Projections.

2016 there will be an increase of 8.5 percent in the total labor force, *thanks in no small part to the participation of older workers.* That is, when the data are disaggregated by age categories, as displayed in the BLS Employment Projections in figure 5, the two *oldest* groups of workers—sixty-five to seventy-four and seventy-five and up—are each expected to grow by more than 80 percent, far outstripping the rate of increase for younger groups (sixteen to twenty-four and twenty-five to fifty-four) and more than twice the rate for fifty-five to sixty-four-year-old workers. In sum, workers age sixty-five and over are expected to constitute 6.1 percent of the total labor force by 2016. And, the BLS remarks, as the ranks swell with the next wave of older workers, the baby boomers, "the graying of the American work force is only just beginning."[25]

Now, having seen how older workers in general are populating the workplace, let us now look at the characteristics of female workers in this age cohort and how and why they are unexpectedly taking greater part in that development.

5

Over Sixty and on the Job

For age is opportunity no less
Than youth itself, though in another dress,
And as the evening twilight fades away
The sky is filled with stars, invisible by day.
—Henry Wadsworth Longfellow, *Morituri Salutamus*, 1875

This chapter lays out general information about the 155 professional women who completed my survey, such as their age, marital and family status, educational achievement, earnings, length of time in the workforce, and so on. Respondents range in age from sixty to eighty-four; their average age is sixty-six. A little more than three-quarters of them are between sixty and sixty-nine years of age, and the rest are seventy and older. They are leading ladies in the dramatic "graying" of the workforce, as discussed in the previous chapter.

Respondents hail from twenty-five states, the District of Columbia, and Dakar, Senegal. Ninety live in New England: Maine, Vermont, Massachusetts, Rhode Island, Connecticut; twenty-eight are from the mid-Atlantic region: New York, New Jersey, Pennsylvania, Washington, D.C., Maryland, Virginia; eleven are from the South: Tennessee, Kentucky, Georgia, South Carolina, Florida, Texas, Mississippi, Arkansas; eight are from the Midwest: Michigan, Illinois, Missouri; and seventeen are from the West and Southwest: California, Colorado, New Mexico, Arizona. Heavily represented are Massachusetts residents (53 percent of the total) and New Yorkers (8 percent).

Marital status has traditionally influenced an older woman's decision whether to enter or continue in the workforce. And it is increasingly common for both husband and wife to be earners (55 percent of married couples of all ages today compared with 44 percent in the late 1960s).[1] More than two-thirds of the survey respondents are married (68 percent); quite a few have been married more than once. Twenty-six of them are currently divorced (17 percent). There are twelve widows (8 percent), almost evenly divided between women in their seventies and eighties and women in their sixties. Eleven women (7 percent) are single. These findings generally follow the direction of national trends concerning the tendency for employed women sixty-five and older to be married. It is interesting to compare the marital status of my survey respondents (*only those sixty-five and older*) with the US BLS Current Population Survey data for that same age group:[2]

BLS: The portion of employed older women who were married in 1977 was about one-third; by 2007 it had increased to nearly half.

My survey: More than two-thirds of respondents sixty-five and older are married, far more than BLS statistics for this age group.

BLS: The portion of employed older women who were widowed, divorced, or separated in 1977 was 56 percent; by 2007 it was 48 percent.

My survey: Many fewer working women sixty-five and older whom I surveyed are widowed or divorced (29 percent).

BLS: The portion that was single in 1977 was 11 percent; by 2007 it was 6 percent.

My survey: Even fewer working women sixty-five and older in my study are single (3 percent).

For some unfathomable reason, my husband was amused when I told him that a considerable number of the older working women responding to my survey had been married two or three times and, in some cases, to a much younger mate after the first or second marriage ended. More power to those women, I was thinking. (I do not even want to speculate about what my husband was thinking.) Why shouldn't women who have deftly maneuvered from one job or career to another potentially better one, as many have chosen or been forced by circumstances to do, also have the freedom to leave a relationship that turned out badly for a healthier, more fulfilling one? Or to choose another partner after becoming a widow?

One woman who has adroitly managed both personal and professional moves is Sharon Caballero. Married for the second time and to a business owner who is younger than she is, Dr. Caballero recently signed on as executive director of the Education Foundation for New Mexico Highlands University after a long career in higher education administration. She and her husband will synchronize their individual retirement decisions when the time comes.

PROFILE: SHARON CABALLERO

When Sharon Caballero was a child, her family was very poor. Her dad was in the military and her mother was at home with seven children. Sharon sewed her own clothes and had but one pair of shoes each year. Her mom was a voracious reader who made sure all her kids had library cards. "We would ride our bikes to the library. We were expected to excel in school and were told that education was the path out of poverty." As the eldest of the seven children, Sharon had many responsibilities, such as diapering the babies. Eventually, five of her brothers and sisters took their first steps to her and said their first words to her. "When I was forty my mom did apologize to me for stealing my childhood," she says wryly. Mom also told Sharon that she did not have to marry and have children to have a good life. Sharon heeded this advice and chose not to have kids of her own. Nevertheless, all the siblings have come to live with her at one time or another, along with their little ones. "So I ended up diapering *their* kids, too!"

A few years after her first marriage ended in divorce, Sharon met and married her second husband, Roger, who is twelve years younger than she is. Through marriage, Sharon acquired two grown stepchildren and two step-grandchildren. The Caballeros live on thirty-seven acres near a small rural hamlet that has just twelve houses and is known as "Old Gophers" in Spanish. The closest town, Sapello, has a mere one hundred houses. Their windows look out at the Sangre de Cristo Mountains, northeast of Santa Fe. They care for a racehorse (it never won a race), two standard horses for trail riding, and two miniatures. Sharon shared with me that when she and Roger first saw each other, "It was love at first sight." They still celebrate every wedding anniversary on New Year's Eve. More routinely, after dinner in the evenings, they do not watch television (and fall asleep on the sofa, as some of us are apt to do); they talk to each other and play games of dominoes called "Mexican Train." Yet, much of the time they are on very different and busy schedules. He owns a plaster and stucco company and she is the executive director of the New Mexico Highlands University Education Foundation.

When Sharon was in her early thirties and teaching high school in Chula Vista, California, one day she realized her brain was turning into a cauliflower. "The cauliflower image was crystal clear: I spoke only in monosyllables in school and what intellect I had was rapidly deteriorating." She took a leave of absence and went for a doctoral degree in education. Armed with new credentials, Sharon then began working her way up the higher education administration career ladder: first as a public relations director of a community college, then as associate director of the statewide California Association of Community Colleges, next as dean at Grossmont Community College in San Diego County, then as vice president at Rio Hondo Community College in Los Angeles, followed by the presidency of San Bernardino Community College for five years. She held top leadership positions in national and state-level associations for women presidents of community colleges.

Her next appointment was to the presidency of New Mexico Highlands University. The university's main campus is in Las Vegas, New Mexico (the *original* Las Vegas, population 14,000). It is a small, comprehensive university with fewer than 4,000 students enrolled at the Las Vegas campus and seven other centers statewide. That job went well for two years until some nasty political shenanigans on the part of the then governor replaced her with one of his cronies, who subsequently went to jail. Forced out, she thought she would try Florida where she was hired to be the president of an online university for two years, but found that she missed New Mexico. She returned there as senior analyst for the state's Legislative Education Study Committee.

While she was on vacation in Hawaii, the mayor of Las Vegas (New Mexico) called to offer her the job of city manager. She took the job, but, unfortunately, the mayor's micromanaging style drove her and other staff members out. Again she received a call—this one in 2009—from the president of the Highlands board, inviting her to come back to the university and head up its foundation. Sharon thought it over—she really liked working, was not ready for volunteer work, felt she still had much to offer (particularly her financial acumen), and liked the recognition that comes with getting a paycheck. She accepted the offer.

At the outset, the ongoing recession made it difficult to raise money and staff salaries had to be frozen. "It is beginning to turn around . . . or maybe I am better at it now! When I was new at this job, my first funding request was for $5,000. Compare that to last week when I shocked myself by asking a prospective donor for ten million dollars with a straight face. And last year I raised the university's largest gift to date: one million dollars."

Although Sharon is glad to have good health and high energy, she finds that she sometimes needs to jump on the stair-stepping machine to get her blood circulating and wake up her brain so she can focus harder on things. "Compared to a college presidency, this line of work is slower paced—it takes time to cultivate relationships and there are fewer staff to help—but I can attain high quality and payoff while appearing to do less."

The very best thing about her job is working in a place she loves with staff she loves. Her proudest accomplishment, however, came when Sharon was vice president at Rio Hondo Community College in East Los Angeles County and she helped persuade California legislators to back the 605 Corridor Project. This was a citizenship education program that enrolled 1 million immigrants. "It was miraculous, a shining moment. We helped to change so many lives!" An amnesty program was then in effect, so undocumented people came forward. Many partner organizations joined the project, as did the federal Immigration and Naturalization Service. The actor Edward James Olmos lent his support.

At sixty-four, Sharon is in the first wave of baby boomers. "It cracks me up to think about it!" she chuckles. Her parents' hair was pure white when they were only in their thirties. Hers is now the same. She had kept her hair blonde for years and the local bankers who became friends of the foundation would call her the "Blonde Bombshell." Now she wears her long hair pulled up in a pony tail and remembers to dress age appropriately. "I tell my husband that I cannot look like when we first met!"

Many of Sharon's friends who are her age or older have already retired. Some of them could afford to retire in their fifties. That did not appeal to Sharon, and she does not anticipate retiring any time soon. "One of the best things about my job is that I get to spend a great deal of time with retired people who are prospective donors to the foundation *and* I am surrounded by so many young people on the campus." When she does step down, she thinks Roger will take early retirement to be in sync with her. Meanwhile, for her sixty-fifth birthday they are going to Waikiki. The romance continues.

All but eighteen of the 155 women in my study have children or stepchildren. Among the 88 percent with children, the number of offspring ranges from one to six. Most common is a family with two or three children, which comports with the average number of children born to married couples nationally in the 1950s, 1960s, and 1970s when my respondents were of child-bearing age. (The average increased from 2.20 children in 1955 to 2.44 children in 1965 then dropped steadily from the late 1970s through the 1990s. It began to climb again in 2008 and was 1.94 children in 2010.)[3]

Professional women need to be well educated, and the survey respondents certainly prove that point. Nearly everyone (95 percent) has at least a bachelor's degree. Three-quarters of the women have a master's, doctorate, or other advanced professional degree, such as an MD or JD. Just under one-half have a master's degree (sometimes two master's or credits beyond the master's). Nearly one-third hold a doctoral degree or other advanced professional degree. The exceedingly impressive accomplishments of these women generally track with trend data discussed in chapter 4 showing ever greater educational achievement for working women.[4]

Early care and education specialist Edna Ranck earned one master's degree after college, shifted direction, and then earned another master's and a doctorate by the time she was fifty. When I interviewed Edna, she was seventy-five years young and enjoying a new job, a remarkably active professional life, and a large extended family. Her story illustrates these educational trends and she continues to work because new and intriguing opportunities keep arising. Here is her story.

PROFILE: EDNA RANCK

A little over a year ago, seventy-five-year-old Edna Ranck took a new job as project director for the Washington Child Development Council (WCDC), the child care resource and referral agency serving the District of Columbia. The council's mission is two-pronged: to help parents and anyone interested in early care and education (ECE) to locate resources, and to guide child care centers and homes through the national accreditation process. Edna oversees a cadre of consultants who facilitate the professional development and staff training that national ECE accreditation requires. Last year she worked full time but now works five fewer hours because of recession-induced funding cuts in the District. She intends to keep working at WCDC as long as the funding holds out.

She is also very active on boards and is past president of the United States chapter of the World Organization for Early Childhood Education, also known as OMEP (Organisation Mondiale pour l'Education Préscolaire). With some fifty years of experience in the pre-K field, she is a respected presenter and panelist at state, national, and international conferences. "I like what I am doing, I get paid to do it, and I have credibility," she says matter-of-factly. Moreover, "it is a way of giving back, it is my legacy." This is also evidenced by the book chapters and articles she has published, with more in the pipeline. Because of her extensive knowledge of the field, the prestigious National Association for the Education of Young Children (NAEYC) recently invited her to co-edit a new column on the history of ECE in the NAEYC journal, *Young Children*. "I was thrilled to be asked to do it. My co-editor is a woman in her forties, representing the next generation. We're calling the column 'Our Proud Heritage.'"

Edna's first advanced degree after college was a master's in divinity from Drew University. She had met a Protestant deaconess who successfully balanced church work and family and Edna thought she could do that too. Starting out as director of a nonprofit preschool in New Jersey in the 1970s, she worked with young children and their teachers and parents. While continuing to work in ECE, she studied for a master's degree and a doctorate in curriculum and teaching and public policy at Columbia University's Teachers College. By then she was fifty years old and her newly minted doctoral degree led to a position at the New Jersey state department of human services.

Along the way, there were personal changes as well. Her first marriage ended and her family merged with that of her second husband, who died in 1979. Her "composed" family now comprises five children and stepchildren, eight grandchildren, one great-grandchild, and a ninety-four-year-old step-mother-in-law.

The family is spread out over two countries, so keeping in touch is a challenge. Edna and her current husband recently celebrated their twenty-eighth anniversary.

Edna does not think she looks "real old." "I wear a size six and dress well, not too youthful, but quite stylish." She admits that her body sometimes says "take it easy," but she still has plenty of stamina. She travels as often as she can, preferably solo, preferably to Paris. Her husband is welcome to come along, but rarely does. He retired after a long career at the Metropolitan Museum of Art in New York City and is very supportive of her extended career. Since her job brought them to Washington, D.C., they often visit the various Smithsonian art galleries and enjoy strolls along the Chesapeake and Ohio Canal towpath from their home in Georgetown.

When I asked Edna whether she is as productive at work as she would like to be, she shot back, "Yes, but there is always more to do!" She is very excited about a whole new area that she recently discovered—media literacy—as it relates to early childhood education. She has joined the advisory board of Reel Fathers, a "daddying" organization founded by educator Allan Shedlin. Reel Fathers (www.reelfathers.com) and its film festival "use the power of cinema and reflective activities to honor and celebrate fathers, and to heal, renew, and deepen the lifelong connection between fathers and children." Edna sees endless possibilities.

Educational attainment usually is an important consideration but not the sole factor in salary decisions. One's professional income can depend on many things besides education, notably part-time versus full-time job status, career field, rank or title, experience level, length of service, performance, ability, and more. Add to the usual salary criteria a severe economic downturn like the one we are currently experiencing and, in spheres lacking contractual protections, one's annual income could easily suffer.

One independent businesswoman characterized her situation this way: "Until 2009 I had many consulting jobs and many companies licensed my software. However, during 2009 my business decreased, probably because of the recession. My only current problem is finding enough work." Another woman, a seventy-one-year-old former social worker and long-time educator who recently found part-time work, wryly comments: "There are few choices for older women re-entering the job market and unless one can command a lucrative consulting fee, the salaries are measly. I think show business and professional sports are the answer for us!"

One of my interviewees, Nancy Bryant, is an active and accomplished older woman who is losing her job because of the recession yet is determined not to be on the shelf. Retirement is definitely out of the question: Nancy became the primary wage earner in her family when her husband retired, and their two sons, who are still in graduate school, need her financial assistance. Fortunately, she loves working and is resilience personified.

PROFILE: NANCY BRYANT

"I am a fixer of systems," seventy-three-year-old Nancy Bryant states confidently. "I wear other people out—they don't move as fast as I do. My mother used to say that about me, too. I see changes that need to be made and have the guts to fight for what I believe in. I am also a follow-through person." Nancy's accomplishments over a fifty-seven-year career back up this claim. She was an effective change agent when she started a program that relocated blind kids in India from residential schools to government-run schools. She had the distinction of being appointed the first female superintendent of a school for the blind in Michigan. And, as an executive with a multicounty Girl Scout Council, she tripled the funding and balanced the budget.

Nancy has always worked. She loves working, especially interacting with people and improving community relations. She has held leadership positions at schools for the blind in several states. There were three "retirements" of short duration because her services have been in constant demand. By the time she went to India, she had already taught school, married, had a child, divorced, earned a doctorate, consulted with the Helen Keller Foundation, and taught at Florida State University. After returning from India with her then eight-year-old son, she remarried, had two more children (after age forty). She and her husband worked in Michigan, New York, and Maryland, and finally settled in Albuquerque, New Mexico. "I fell in love with Albuquerque. I am very involved in the community, for example, volunteering in the Assistance League thrift shop and participating in a domestic violence network. We still have a farm in Michigan, though, so we go back and forth."

For the past year, Nancy has been administering a Strengthening Families initiative for the Cooperative Extension Service at New Mexico State University. The program, founded a decade ago in the Las Cruces area and now centered in Albuquerque (the state's major population center), helps parents help their children, for example, teaching fathering skills and working with teen moms. Professional development is important to her: she will attend a conference on healthy marriages and classes on attachment disorders in children; she also makes time for mentoring a young female intern. Unfortunately, the program she administers will lose its grant funding because of the recession and the state's dire financial situation, and Nancy expects to lose her job. Seven staffers will be laid off.

Ever resilient, she is networking in hopes of finding a job. Aware that age discrimination could be an obstacle, she is relieved that it may be less of a problem in the university milieu. Retirement is simply not an option for now: two sons still in graduate school depend on her for financial assistance. Her husband retired at sixty-five, making Nancy the primary wage earner in the family. "I have told my husband and kids that age seventy-five might be a reasonable target for retirement. It really depends whether I still love what I am doing and can do it well."

She finds the spiritual and introspective sides of her personality emerging. "Is what I *do* who I *am*?" she wonders. "Do my accomplishments define who I am? Do I need to work so hard? I could be busy with other things, like artistic pursuits or traveling to Australia and New Zealand." Still, she has not forgotten that the women of her era fought to get where they are, and that also motivates her to keep working and to keep acting as a role model.

Reflecting on her childhood in a WASP-y family in Miami, Nancy recalls her doting father, a physician, encouraging her to get a good education. "He was handsome, energetic, charismatic, and outdoorsy. I stuck to him like glue." Her personality is much like his—she loves scuba diving, hiking, and camping—and she attributes her good health to being so active. Her mother was very different. When her husband died young and she had to support the family, she made it clear that Nancy's brother would get preference for a college education. Nancy had to put herself through school. Only now that Nancy is older has she come to appreciate and emulate her mother's good qualities, her commitment to community service, and her domestic interests, gardening and sewing. And she's thankful that her mother taught her to use cold cream—it keeps her looking younger than her years!

Nancy would like to inspire younger women (and her granddaughters when they are old enough to understand) with the following advice: stay healthy; look ahead; think hard about your goals and do not get sidetracked by a partner who holds you back; be well educated; make good choices so you work at something that is really satisfying (not just drudgery); and plan to live to be one hundred or more!

To find out how well older women are faring salary-wise in the workforce, the survey asked respondents to indicate current personal income in one of three categories: "modest" (under $30,000), "middle" ($30,000 to $79,000), or "higher" ($80,000 and up).[5] All but five of the full-time and part-time workers were willing to share information about their salary range. Their personal incomes are fairly evenly spread across the categories: 28 percent report modest income, 36 percent have middle incomes, and 36 percent enjoy higher income. Women between sixty and sixty-nine tend to earn in the middle and higher ranges, while women seventy and older tend to earn in the modest and middle ranges. This difference can partially be explained by the higher incidence of part-time work among women seventy and older, time taken out for raising a family, as well as a propensity for starting over in a new job or career after leaving a previous longer-term position. It is also related to choice of occupational field and access (or lack thereof) to higher-paying jobs.

Notably, regardless of age or field, more than half of the respondents with full-time jobs (58 percent) are earning more than $80,000 per year. Owing most likely to their professional or managerial status,[6] this income level far exceeds the median earnings of all full-time older workers as reported by the US BLS. Even if the income of these older women still lags behind men's, it certainly compares quite favorably with the peak earning years for baby boomers and surely offers some protection against the financial troubles besetting so many Americans. Their economic status may also be associated with residence in the New England and mid-Atlantic states where the majority of my survey respondents live, since the District of Columbia (where government and public sector jobs abound), Maryland, Massachusetts, and Connecticut, have the highest rates of professional and managerial women and the highest annual earnings for full-time, year-round employed women.[7]

To be sure, education has more than monetary value for women. An African proverb that Greg Mortenson is fond of reciting in his best-selling books *Three Cups of Tea* and *Stones into Schools* says: "If you teach a boy, you educate an individual; but if you teach a girl, you educate a community." When educated girls grow up they are likely to dedicate themselves to helping others, and they often excel at building relationships which in turn can facilitate social change. For these reasons, Mortenson argues, girls' education is a "force multiplier."[8] As we shall see in the next chapter, many of the well-educated older working women whom I surveyed are, like ECE specialist Edna Ranck, engaged in the "helping" professions.

On average, survey respondents have been working for forty years. The number of years worked overall ranged from ten (low) to sixty-three (high). More than half of the women had taken time out for child rearing (58 percent), but among the most highly educated women in my survey (those with doctoral or other professional degrees), only 39 percent had taken time out for child rearing. (Some of these high-achieving women may have been fortunate enough to have family or friends or paid help who provided child care.) Women seventy and older were more likely to have taken time out for child rearing than women in their sixties—69 percent compared to 54 percent. The trend away from the "stay-at-home mom" was just beginning when the latter group was deciding whether to enter the workforce. It is now in full force: nearly three-quarters of married mothers in this country are in the labor market today, and financial dependence on one's spouse, once the norm, has been replaced by the two-income family.[9] (The percentage in the labor market is lower for moms with children under the age of six and higher for those whose youngest child is between six and seventeen.[10])

Time out of the workforce is not reserved for parenting of young children. Traditionally, women have also been seen as adult caregivers and, willingly or unwillingly, have taken responsibility for elderly or disabled family members.[11] However, only 4 percent of my survey respondents said they had actually taken time out for adult care or were doing so presently. Still others were able to help look after elderly or disabled family members without incurring any career interruptions or had the resources to hire help.

These enterprising women are managing to make aging and working compatible. Mulling over that idea, we can thank Gail Sheehy and writers who came after her for a whole new lexicon for discussing aging. In *New Passages,* Sheehy sets out to help readers make sense of their own lives by understanding the lives of men and women across the adult life span.[12] She recalls "the conventional maps" our parents followed and the "timetables" that went with them—adulthood starting at twenty-one and ending at sixty-five. Instead of the old map, Sheehy says, her subjects were enjoying a Second Adulthood with newfound vitality even as they "were also getting older, lumpier, bumpier, slower, and closer to the end."[13] She divides this period into two major stages: the "Age of Mastery" (forty-five to sixty-five) and the "Age of Integrity" (sixty-five to eighty-five, and older). The latter stage, referring to a process of integrating the various elements and roles in one's life, "bringing all the parts into harmony and becoming more authentic,"[14] readily applies to the women I studied.

All in all, my findings generally reinforce Sheehy's insightful appraisal of people in the Age of Integrity who "continue to work in one way or another—part time, or as consultants, contract teachers, community volunteers, or self-employed entrepreneurs—not only because they want to feel a sense of purpose or self-worth but because they will have to be prepared to support themselves for greatly elongated lives."[15] And I agree that the old maps and timetables in use even as recently as a decade and a half ago when *New Passages* was published no longer adequately define the lives of older professional women.

However, I see one important distinction between Sheehy's subjects and mine. Instead of what Sheehy describes as "hurtling along the edge" of an unknown precipice separating youth and old age, the women I surveyed are progressing steadily and deliberately along their chosen paths. I am reminded of Ma Joad's observation in *The Grapes of Wrath* that a woman looks at life as "all in one flow, like a stream, little eddies, little waterfalls, but the river, it goes right on," allowing her to move along more nimbly than a man. My subjects, already sixty-plus and only partially resigned to increasing lumpiness and bumpiness, spottiness, and occasionally a moment of dotty-ness, are concentrating on their work and trying to fit in some leisure, not looking to wholly reinvent themselves at this point in their lives. As my friend and special educator MaryAnn DiGiovanni puts it, the challenge is balancing work and the rest of one's life, knowing that the balance changes over time.

The women I studied seem to have achieved a high degree of autonomy or what Sheehy refers to as a "firm sense of self."[16] This is not to say that they do not explore and change at all, simply that there is less daring than Sheehy envisions. Transitioning very gradually from "young-old" to "old-old," they are hardly ignorant of or frightened by next steps or new challenges. They seem quite self-assured and enjoying the stability, constancy, and rewards of their working lives. Let's turn next to their career choices and job status.

6

Where Older Women Work

"[N]eed a fresh map of life, a new course that extends productivity much deeper into lives" for those able to keep working.—Marc Freedman, *Encore: Finding Work That Matters in the Second Half of Life*

Though young women today can choose among a multitude of career fields, heretofore career choices for young women were severely limited. With few prospects for making headway in such domains as banking, publishing, medicine, and law, they typically flocked to the so-called helping professions in the 1960s and 1970s where doors were wide open to women.[1] Small wonder then that the greatest number of professional women I surveyed have careers in education, health care, social work, or social services, as well as in business and the arts. Not so coincidentally, this list coincides with jobs projected to increase over the next eight years in the United States in education, health care, government, and nonprofit organizations, such as the arts, museums, and libraries.[2] Even in these fields, however, the recession is taking a toll—teachers laid off and library hours and staff reduced.

While professional and managerial women are working in a great variety of career fields, education is number one among survey respondents. Well over one-third (39 percent) are educators, most holding positions in higher education, K–12, or early childhood teaching and administration, as well as in educational therapy. A few are freelance instructors, for example, teaching bridge or watercolor classes, or giving workshops on services to the visually impaired. Just under one-quarter of the women are in business. Twelve percent are in health care. Practitioners and administrators in social work or social services represent 8 percent. Six percent are in the arts—music, theater, dance, painting, museum work, and conservation. And among the rest are five fundraisers; four librarians; three ministers; two lawyers; a researcher for the federal government, state governments, and foundations; and a federal government administrator.

Higher education is Barbara Millis's milieu. Barbara directs the Teaching and Learning Center at the University of Texas at San Antonio and, like Nancy Bryant and others in my study, is the primary breadwinner in her family. Highly regarded in her field, at sixty-five she anticipates many more productive years in the workforce. While financial exigencies are holding her in the workforce, it's the opportunities to keep learning and be creative that make continuing to work most appealing.

PROFILE: BARBARA MILLIS

Barbara Millis has had a long career in higher education. After her husband earned his doctorate in English literature, they taught overseas and traveled all over Asia for nine years. Barbara finished her doctorate in English literature and composition from Florida State University while they were teaching in Misawa, Japan. When they returned stateside, Barbara taught at the University of Maryland/University College, the United States Air Force Academy, and the University of Nevada at Reno. Three years ago she was hired by the University of Texas at San Antonio (UTSA). With higher education's burgeoning interest in improving college teaching and learning, she has directed faculty development programs at each campus. She is especially proud of her success in orchestrating the process by which the United States Air Force Academy was selected by the Association of American Colleges and Universities as one of sixteen leadership institutions in undergraduate education nationwide.

Barbara earns research and teaching awards, serves as an executive editor for a journal on college teaching, and writes books (a total of four published, with two in progress), articles, and chapters for publication. Active in the Professional and Organizational Development Network in Higher Education, she advises rookie faculty developers and is in constant demand as a consultant to other universities across the country and as a conference keynote speaker. Therefore, it came as a shock when the president of the University of Nevada at Reno abruptly closed her faculty development program, and she was out of a job.

Although upset by the unexpected closure and anxious about re-entering the job market during the recession, Barbara need not have worried. Her reputation as one of the top faculty developers in the country stood her in good stead; she soon had five solid job offers. In 2008, she was appointed full-time director of the Teaching and Learning Center (TLC) at UTSA, a San Antonio campus with 17,000 students and 1,200 faculty members. She was able to hit the ground running—working with faculty and teaching assistants on teaching, assessment, and publication enhancements, and mentoring and coaching a cadre of ten university teaching fellows (graduate students selected by a committee from various departments). "Since my staff is quite small, the fellows are my salvation. They are simply a joy to work with." Fellows make classroom observations, conduct specialized focus groups, consult about instructional matters, and help support teaching award nominees.

Barbara's first love is facilitating workshops, particularly sessions that focus on cooperative learning, her specialty. "I'm almost evangelical about workshops!" she confesses. "Workshops can be highly effective in transforming how faculty teach, and that, in turn, allows them to reach their students." What is most exciting for her are "breakthroughs" at workshops, insights about instruction that are career changing in their influence. "I emphasize the theories behind learner-centered practices without hammering faculty with footnotes! I am careful to 'practice what I preach' by modeling classroom management approaches."

Barbara served for two years as a tri-chair for UTSA's United Way Campaign, setting records for donations, and also serves on university-wide committees, including those that address institutional leadership, teaching, and accreditation. (To earn accreditation, every university in the South must have a so-called quality enhancement plan. UTSA's plan, which focuses on quantitative literacy across the curriculum, involves the TLC.)

Barbara intends to keep working. She feels as though she has to stay "in harness." She and her husband have been paying for two mortgages (with Nevada's extreme recession and real estate glut, they are unable to sell the Reno house) plus their daughter's expensive art school tuition and her wedding in 2011. "The mortgages are a terrible drain," Barbara sighs. "Luckily, I really love my work and I'm blessed with good health." Barbara recently recovered from a total knee replacement after hurting herself while whitewater rafting in Colorado—she was in Leadville serving as a faculty mentor at Boot Camp for Profs.

What Barbara most appreciates about her job are the constant opportunities to learn from research and from the people she meets and the places she visits. "I'm always curious about new ideas, always synthesizing. I see connections between creative ideas and try to put them together to benefit my institution. For example, I'm working on the synergy between our quality enhancement plan and a National Science Foundation–funded initiative involving economics—what links them is their emphasis on quantitative thinking. I am also fascinated by the connections between cooperative learning, deep learning, and the research on how people learn."

What Barbara doesn't like about higher education institutions is the possibility of running into a political buzz saw, the kind she experienced firsthand in Reno when her center was shut down despite having given it her all. She has taken a poem by e. e. cummings as her mantra: "i sing of Olaf glad and big" celebrates a man who bravely defies convention, endures cruel mistreatment, and yet never loses his dignity. Olaf's endurance appears to speak volumes to this spirited woman.

The second most popular career field for my respondents is business. Women are working in the following fields: finance, real estate, travel, tax preparation, telecommunications, corporate training, human resources, technology, sales, secretarial, marketing, publishing, and design. We can take human resources manager Charlotte B. of Tennessee as an example. Running the Employee Relations Department for a large restaurant chain with 14,500 employees in twenty states is the latest stop along Charlotte's career path.

Luckily for the company that depends on her, she has no interest in retiring for quite some time.

PROFILE: CHARLOTTE B.

Charlotte B. is happiest when her "bucket is full" and she is using her brain. She does not like being idle. "I personally love working and feel validation every day, even after thirty years in the workforce. I took a ten-year break when raising children, and a couple of years off here and there since, and nearly went stark raving mad. . . . It is true," she goes on, "that sometimes I am under a lot of pressure at work. Since the economy resulted in a reduction in force two years ago, I have been the only person running the Employee Relations Department for a large restaurant chain with 14,500 employees in twenty states. (There used to be four people handling a work load for ten.) On the other hand, I get a lot of positive support, at least mentally and emotionally, from my coworkers and from company leadership, who encourage me and openly express how much they value me and my work. I deal with a lot of negative situations, but I try to be upbeat and use humor when I can."

For seven years, Charlotte has investigated and resolved sensitive workplace harassment, discrimination, retaliation, and wage and hour complaints from her office at company headquarters in Nashville. She walks managers and hourly employees through the grievance process and explains their legal rights as construed by the federal Equal Employment Opportunity Commission. Given her area of expertise, she would know age or gender discrimination if it was directed her way; yet, with a boss and company higher-ups who are female and decades younger, that is not a problem for her. Anyway, she does not feel old (at sixty-five) and coworkers, all younger, do not perceive her as old. "Sometimes I do not relate to what they are chitchatting about," she admits, "but, most importantly, I am energized by being part of a wonderful corporate structure in a culture that is supportive of its employees. What is more, I work in a climate where *what* you do is important and how you present yourself is how you are perceived and rewarded. It is not about age or gender."

Charlotte describes her career history as "a long and winding road." Before entering the human resources field she taught high school English for many years and was a technical writer. During two periods of temporary unemployment along the way, boredom plagued her. She did not enjoy meeting friends for coffee and listening to them complaining endlessly about their lives. Her husband put his finger on the problem: "You're not *you* anymore. You need to use your mind and get involved in something meaningful."

"I think that some of my contentment is because I have such a loving, understanding, and supportive spouse. He's fourteen years younger and also has a very demanding job as a programmer analyst and developer." They both come home tired out at night after a long day. She expects to retire before he does—having time to try her hand at creative writing is a lure—but that is not going to happen for a while because, if she did, their lives would be out of sync. Her grown children are proud of her too (they think their mom is terrific), but they live far away and are busy with their own jobs and kids. Hence her strong commitment to the company, at least for another four or five years.

Charlotte describes herself as very independent, highly productive, and a quick learner, especially with respect to technology. She inherited these qualities from her mother who, after raising a family, worked until she was sixty-five. After that, however, her mother became "clingy" and dependent on her husband. That was not the path Charlotte chose. "I have always taken a lot on myself, and I do not depend on others for a sense of worth."

Charlotte readily acknowledges, "I am happy in my sandbox." Her philosophy, too, is upbeat: whether you are working by choice or out of financial necessity, come to work with a smile—it helps you get through the day. "While the current economy has somewhat affected my finances, I do not worry about it. When my first marriage broke up and I was a single mom, I really needed the money. As I have gotten older, I depend less on my job for the income it provides. My goal now is helping the company, being effective. I could retire today and be quite comfortable, but I do not plan to retire until (a) the company decides it is time for me to go, or (b) I can't remember my name!"

Neither of those situations is likely to occur, however. For one thing, the company cannot get along without her. Her bosses panic when she goes on vacation twice a year. As of now, she chuckles, "I am still in the game. I may even get a promotion!"

Health care, another of the female-dominated career fields, employs several of the women in medicine and nursing. One of the older women with a highly challenging job on the business side of the health care industry, Ginger Burrus, refused to let gender stereotypes interfere with her education and astute career moves. Now she is working hard and fears she would be bored if she stopped. Owing to the downturn in the economy and the need for health care coverage, she is unlikely to retire anytime soon.

PROFILE: GINGER BURRUS

"Creative and analytic" is how a colleague describes Ginger Burrus. Those polarities nicely capture the often contradictory thoughts she has about her work and retirement. She has worked in various management and problem solving roles for nearly twenty-four years at a large health care organization in Colorado where currently she is Senior Manager, Business Intelligence Solutions—Data Governance and Quality. She oversees a department that performs data warehousing, the integration of data from multiple business and clinical systems to promote quality and standards so that data can be used to drive decisions about company business.

At sixty-three, Ginger's plans for retirement are quite fluid. She vacillates between staying on the job one to three years longer or retiring to the vacation home with the "jaw-dropping" view of the mountains and having time for drawing and painting classes, hiking and biking, and entertaining friends. Between loving the intellectual challenge of her work and dreading that boredom might set in if she stops. Between mentoring bright co-workers yet knowing she is decades older than they are. Between feeling healthy, energetic, and open to new ideas and admitting that her long daily commute is taking a toll.

"I was not even thinking about retirement until my staff began to tell me I must not retire because they need me. What prompted them to say that? It has changed my perception of myself. I am beginning to sense that age is creeping in. Maybe it is time to pass the torch." Then again, if an exciting new job opportunity presented itself, she would definitely reconsider.

Ginger's husband is a psychologist in private practice. "He absolutely supports my decision to keep working because I have the steady income and carry the health insurance for both of us. The financial piece has taken on greater importance recently what with the downturn in the economy and the need for health care coverage. That's just the way it is."

Ginger is a self-made woman who somehow never thought that anything could hold her back. Growing up, she knew she wanted to be an engineer, but no one encouraged her to get an education or have a career. Her father did not want her to go to college, and he informed her that girls could *not* be engineers. "His attitude profoundly influenced my eventual academic and career paths," she says matter-of-factly. Ginger first worked in a Washington, D.C., hospital to pay for most of her undergraduate training in medical technology. In her thirties, she resolved to take a master's degree in biostatistics and that led to a succession of interesting career moves, including the opportunity to help design a new hospital.

Ginger is interested in what other older women are thinking about their careers, about aging and retirement. Are they as mesmerized as she is by the yin and yang of life, and how interdependent it all is? In the business arena with which she is most familiar, she knows few females in her own age group who are well educated and engaged in professional careers. Women her age who are working are usually administrative assistants. Most of her professional friends are boomers five to ten years younger than she is, leading her to wonder if her generation missed the boat career-wise. "It is a fascinating question!"

Another woman who chose her own way despite many obstacles is Amy Kaiser, full-time chorus director of the Saint Louis Symphony Orchestra. She expects her highly successful career in the arts to continue indefinitely. Amy is one of the relatively few women holding artistic leadership positions in the classical music field, and she would like to still be working when that is no longer the norm.

PROFILE: AMY KAISER

"Miraculously, it all worked out for me," marvels Amy Kaiser, full-time chorus director of the Saint Louis Symphony Orchestra. Her parents, both educators, were products of the Depression; they wanted her to choose a safe and secure profession and earn a pension like they did. Her father, now going on 105, retired from his job as an elementary school principal at sixty-five and is enjoying happy, productive elder years. Contrary to her parents' wishes, Amy followed her muse and chose music, historically an *insecure* profession. Miracle or not, she is the only full-time female chorus director for a major orchestra in this country and probably internationally.

She is single and has no regrets about that, believing she could not have accomplished all she has if she had a family. Moreover, she is unique. While women have made tremendous strides in other fields, very few women hold positions of artistic leadership in the classical music profession. Many women play in orchestras today and a few are conducting. Women are successful orchestra executives, too. There are many female choral directors in schools and colleges, but they are not employed by major orchestras.

Amy understands insecurity. The Saint Louis Symphony almost went bankrupt ten years ago, but with new, enlightened leadership, major gifts from generous Saint Louisans, and much dedication and hard work, the endowment and the audiences have been rebuilt. Now, despite the recession, the symphony is thriving, and luckily, even without tenure, Amy feels secure.

However, that was not the case during the many years she was a freelance conductor in New York City. As a young woman forty years ago she directed the choral music program at State University of New York at Stony Brook, then left academe for part-time positions at the Mannes College of Music and the 92nd Street Y in Manhattan. In quick succession (and sometimes at the same time) she conducted the Dessoff Choirs in performances at Lincoln Center; conducted operas for children with the Metropolitan Opera Guild; led numerous operatic and choral world premieres; and prepared choruses for the New York Philharmonic and Mostly Mozart Festival. She was a faculty member at the Manhattan School of Music and led educational concerts for the New York Chamber Symphony at the 92nd Street Y. "I was in the middle of things in one of the exciting musical capitals of the world, but I had no health insurance, was doing too much work, and was getting older," she recalls. "I needed a full-time job with benefits, and for that, I had to relocate." Fifteen years ago she found what she was looking for in Saint Louis. "I traded the autonomy I had known as a freelancer to become a team player on an 'A-level' team."

The transition was difficult. Gradually, Amy bought a house and a grand piano, learned to garden, began working out with a personal trainer to stay fit, and set about making all new friends in Saint Louis. In addition to her directorial duties, she guest conducted at the Grant Park and Berkshire Choral Festivals and taught choral conducting in master classes and workshops. She did try to cut back. However, about seven years ago, a friend arranged for Amy to teach a private class on opera for adults. That class was popular and soon morphed into two groups—the Symphony Lecture Series and the Saint Louis Opera Club, each sixty-strong. "With my mostly manageable schedule of contact hours, that has become a very rewarding companion piece to my primary job."

Age is not an issue in the Saint Louis Symphony. Some members of the orchestra and staff are older than her mere sixty-five. On the other hand, executives on the business side of the organization are typically in their mid-thirties and "technologically in a different world," she muses. She did experience age discrimination in New York City—"a shocker, an eye-opener. I lost a precious freelance job because of that," she recalls.

The most meaningful part of Amy's job is the day-to-day work of making music with 130 very talented singers in the Saint Louis Symphony Chorus. She enjoys interacting with everyone in the organization, working in a beautiful hall, and hearing beautiful music made by her colleagues. Not only must she meet her own exacting standards, she must also meet the standards of the orchestra's acclaimed music director, David Robertson. The stakes are high. Robertson often selects exceptionally challenging scores, such as works by American composer John Adams and Central European composer György Ligeti, in addition to the standard repertoire. Amy is proud of the results from the chorus. When she started working in Saint Louis fifteen years ago, it was a very good chorus. Now it is outstanding. Robertson, guest conductors, members of the orchestra, and audiences praise the sound and musical quality.

One guest conductor said he came to Saint Louis expecting to find a world-class orchestra and did; he did not know he would be working with a world-class chorus as well. Honorifics from another direction came in the form of recognition as a "Remarkable Woman" by her *alma mater* Smith College (along with Julia Child, Betty Freidan, and Gloria Steinem) and the Smith College Medal for outstanding professional achievement in 2004.

The manageable schedule and the rewarding work make her want to continue on indefinitely with the Saint Louis Symphony. She would teach more if she could share her expertise with aspiring conductors. "I made a smart move at age fifty. I downsized to one big job from seven." She has always loved her work and hopes to continue well into her seventies, if possible, or as long as she remains healthy and energetic. "Why stop?" she queries. Hiking in Glacier, Bryce, and Zion National Parks and river rafting and trekking with other wilderness-seekers in Alaska are favorite activities. "I've budgeted to age ninety, but that might not be enough, given my Dad's track record," she quips.

A plethora of titles describes the professional women I studied. For example, in education they are professor, teacher, instructor, dean, interpreter, tutor, and director. In business they are president, owner, principal, manager, coordinator, supervisor, executive director, bookkeeper, paymaster, trainer, financial planner, writer, and editor. In social services they are therapist, social worker, counselor, and psychologist.

Two-thirds of these professional women are working in the private sector, the remainder in the public sphere (29 percent), or both public and private (6 percent). More than two-thirds hold jobs in a metropolitan area. Twenty-eight percent are working in nonmetropolitan locales and 5 percent work in both metropolitan and nonmetropolitan areas. On the whole, professional work has always been easier to find in metropolitan areas. However, the recession has weakened that premise, at least temporarily.[3] Salaries also tend to be higher for urban workers than for workers in nonmetropolitan areas in the same occupations.[4]

Whether by personal choice or, more likely, by financial necessity, 17 percent of my respondents also have a *second* job today. Some of these are: after-school program counselor, church treasurer, tree farmer, actress, consultant, private practitioner, artist, substitute school nurse, and online salesperson. The tree farmer raises and sells Christmas trees with her husband as a side business; her primary business is running a real estate agency and she is a tree farmer by choice rather than out of necessity. The after-school counselor and the others have second jobs to bring in a little more money.

One woman who leads house-building projects in developing countries for Habitat for Humanity told me that she considers it to be her second job. I thought she was leading the tours for financial reasons, that is, to supplement her salary as an elementary school art teacher, but I found that I was mistaken when she explained her primary reason for undertaking the work—it seems she took to heart her yoga instructor's admonition to "take one step toward the universe and the universe will respond in kind." Although she receives no salary for her "second job," she benefits from seeing the world, knowing that she is helping others, and acquiring new materials and ideas to use in her classroom.

PROFILE: MARGIE SISITSKY

Margie Sisitsky's full-time job is teaching art at the same high-need, low-income elementary school I taught in in the 1980s. (She is also the twin sister of Merry Glosband, who was introduced in chapter 4.) When the school received an influx of Brazilian students a decade ago, this highly experienced and dedicated art teacher thought she should immerse herself in Brazilian culture to work more effectively with her students. She signed up for Habitat for Humanity and, in the summer of 2001, joined a team of volunteer house builders assigned to Brazil. That was the first of seven Habitat for Humanity trips she has taken to developing countries. Her next Habitat trip, still as a team member, took her to a remote corner of Ghana. She then decided to enroll in Habitat's required leadership training course to become a team leader. In that capacity, she has taken teams to the southernmost tip of India, the mountains of Thailand, Ulan Bator in Mongolia, and along the Mekong Delta in Vietnam. In the summer of 2011 Margie led a team to the Philippines. "It has become a little addictive," she confides.

Margie chose some of the destinations because she had been completing professional development work and wanted to learn more about the countries. She selected Thailand because she thought the food would be especially good there. She went to the Philippines because she knows several Filipinos and "something seemed to be pushing me there."

"It is a ton of work, but always a rewarding and enriching experience. It is challenging on many levels." She is responsible for interviewing all the prospective team members and finding out why they want to participate; leading team building activities to bring them together and keep them focused on teamwork; making arrangements for room and board (they could be staying in a hotel or with a local family and cooking over a charcoal fire or dining in a restaurant). The tour leader and team members each pay about $1,700 plus airfare for a two-week trip. Habitat for Humanity does not pay Margie a salary for her work; she has to pay her own way (her four children and their spouses have contributed, and a small assessment from team members helps to defray her expenses).

Her Flat Stanley doll travels with Margie on every trip. (*Flat Stanley*, a 1964 children's book written by Jeff Brown, features Stanley Lambchop, a completely flat boy.) To share her experiences with her students, she takes pictures of the well-traveled doll to pin to the bulletin boards in her classroom, along with the flags of the countries she has visited and words in the language of the country. Even though Margie does not get a salary, she feels she is more than repaid by the opportunity to do meaningful work in fascinating places with her team and then share it all with her students come September.

It is now easier to continue working as long as one wishes in many jobs, especially in higher education. My husband, for one, is seventy-five, a professor of history and humanities at a nearby university, and a publishing historian. And, although I did say in chapter 1 that older men's distinctive stories will have to wait for a follow-up investigation, I think you will understand why I could not resist including the following snapshot of an older man who has three jobs and is my husband's college friend, Ed Myers.

Ed is eighty years old (he served in the Navy before attending college). He is blessed with good health and high energy and is still working thirty-five, or more, hours per week in three part-time positions. He is a sales manager for a computer services company in Austin, Texas—an Austin-area staffing agency called Senior Work Solutions found the job for him. He is a swimming instructor and lifeguard for the local YMCA, *and* he is a professional model for television commercials and print advertisements. Ed told me that he expects to continue working at least another six years—he really enjoys working and staying busy. Oh, and he also volunteers his time teaching a swimming and water exercise class for Alzheimer's patients in the YMCA's Senior Retreat program. Ed was recently featured in an *Austin Statesman* article[5] about working after retirement and how that can bring fulfillment and financial security, but in truth, he has never really retired. The parts about fulfillment and financial security are certainly accurate: Ed gets satisfaction from using his experience and skills in all three jobs, and, with the economy the way it is, the extra money he earns comes in handy when he and his wife want to travel.

Let's get back to the women's stories. As a full-time college professor who responded to my survey says, "I'm sixty-nine and I do think about retirement, but I still enjoy my teaching, love my students, feel that I'm very helpful to my colleagues and the college, and appreciate the income, so I'm still working." Yet another college professor who has the same upbeat attitude about her work is seventy-nine-year-old Karel Rose. She told me that she finds working with her Brooklyn College students to be both energizing and surprising. Her husband also seems to be fulfilled by his work—at ninety-one he is teaching dental students at New York University.

PROFILE: KAREL ROSE

Karel Rose has worked fifty-one years, the past forty-one years as professor of education, English, and women's studies at the City University of New York/ Brooklyn College and the Graduate Center. She loves teaching—children's literature, philosophy, and women's studies classes—for which she has won many awards. At seventy-eight she started a blog and holds Socrates Cafes (informal gatherings where participants engage in philosophical inquiry) to encourage students and alumni to think about and debate such topics as: happiness, wisdom, what it means to live well, and why civility is essential to society. Karel also advises students, mentors new faculty, and serves on the Tenure and Promotion Committee of the college.

The student body at Brooklyn College is tremendously varied; more than six dozen languages are spoken on campus. She not only finds working with students to be energizing, it is also surprising—she uses the word deliberately—because as we age it is easy to lose one's sense of wonder and capacity for being surprised. Teaching is a very hopeful way to live one's life, she believes, for knowledge is a bottomless process and it is incredibly exciting to always be learning. "I won't retire," she says, "until I get the hang of it. I'm still trying to get it right." It gives her great joy to know that she may be positively affecting her students. Karel also lectures around the country on women's issues and has given papers and lectured in Bhutan, Central America, Turkey, Germany, and Poland. "Being an academic is enormously gratifying. I don't know what I would do if I lost my health or couldn't drive and had to stop working." None of Karel's close friends outside of Brooklyn College are working; some of them regret that they retired because they have concerns about how to fill their time. That is not likely to be a problem for her. She is already writing another book, this one on resilience, how people cope with adversity in their lives.

Karel describes her husband as "enormously cooperative from day one." With his unwavering support, she earned a doctoral degree in black literature, pioneering work in 1969, while raising five sons ("oooh, those stinky sneakers—I lived in a men's locker room for years!"). It wasn't easy: she depended upon cooperation from other mothers in the neighborhood and was fortunate enough to be able to afford hired help. Now ninety-one years young, her husband is teaching at NYU's dental school after a long and successful career in dentistry. He was the youngest of eight children. His siblings all lived to a ripe old age, though now the whole large family is gone. "Our social world is continually shrinking," Karel notes pensively.

Karel and her husband have a second home in Lenox, Massachusetts, near Tanglewood, the summer home of the Boston Symphony Orchestra, and close to a luxury health spa and resort where Karel has been giving workshops for twenty years, encouraging women to "have a clear-eyed view of the human predicament and honor your own authenticity. Trust your gut. Recognize your *inner* beauty, for what is external soon fades. Feel genuine about your work (paid or not) or whatever you do, and you'll be fine." Karel swims, walks, and meditates to "quiet the chatter in my head."

"Maybe I'm in denial—I'm a very 'up' person and I don't always notice the negatives in my life. I drive two hours a day to Brooklyn College, enjoy working at my desk at home, take four-mile walks as often as I can, and swim, swim, swim. I'm really fortunate, and I am grateful for that." Karel has eight grandchildren living all over the country, so she visits and helps out sometimes but cannot be a full-time grandmother. The recession has not played havoc with her life, but she does worry about her children's financial future and is concerned about the kind of world her grandchildren will inherit. "Maybe my generation had the best of it," she says.

Karel added that she thoroughly enjoyed the interview: "It makes me explore the maps in my head depicting life's journey. I'm thinking about the necessary losses that inevitably come with age and hope that I may be growing a bit wiser. That's the nice part of aging. It may be easier for women who experience satisfying careers—a life devoted to asking the kinds of questions that elude simple answers is wonderful preparation for the shock of accepting one's mortality. Plus, one no longer has to do it all. It's now easier to take a pass on perfection, sit back a bit and reflect. I hope Picasso was right when he said, 'We start to get young past sixty.'"

Self-employment, consulting, and business ownership make it far easier to continue working and to maintain earning power. Indeed, the *New York Times* recently published a special section on retirement featuring men and women fifty-five or older who were not ready to retire and decided to set up their own businesses. No doubt the information is timely not only for the leading edge of baby boomers, but also for even older folks for whom self-employment is a way to parlay their considerable know-how, skills, experience, and contacts into a new venture. They have the desire and confidence to go out on their own, provided, of course, they are able to meet clients' or customers' needs. According to the Small Business Association, more than five million Americans fifty-five or older are running their own businesses or otherwise self-employed. The association says the number of self-employed people fifty-five to sixty-four soared 52 percent from 2000 to 2007. The Center for Retirement Research at Boston College agrees that there has been an entrepreneurial spurt, but says it occurred after mid-2008.[6]

Renee Solomon, the self-employed seventy-nine-year-old therapist whom you are about to meet in the next profile, feels as strongly about her independence as her private practice. From personal experience she knows that a woman has to fight for her place in society when she is aging; it is easier for a man. She is indignant about the way older women are often ignored. When she declares that women want to be recognized (i.e., to count), I am reminded of a passage from Catherine Schine's new book, *The Three Weissmanns of*

Westport, describing older women retaining beauty and vibrancy as they age but experiencing "irrelevance."[7]

PROFILE: RENEE SOLOMON

Seventy-nine-year-old Renee Solomon knew she wanted to be a social worker from her earliest days in the Brownsville section of Brooklyn when she lived next door to a settlement house. Her mother, a Russian immigrant, sent Renee there to play and learn to be "American." The social workers at the Hebrew Educational Society taught her to play basketball and socialized her. The chairwoman of the settlement house board saw leadership potential in the girl and took her under her wing. Renee still remembers being escorted to the Brooklyn Academy of Music to hear Mozart's opera, *Cosi fan tutte*. Under the influence of both male and female settlement workers, she made plans to go to college, the first in her family ever to do so, and become a social worker. She aimed to work *with* and *for* people. "There was never any question."

One of her favorite mentors at the settlement house drummed into her an adage she has tried to live by: "Be a good doer, not a do-gooder." Her mentor went on to join the faculty at Columbia University's School of Social Work. She too went to Columbia, first to earn a master's degree and then, some twenty years later, as a faculty member. Married to an engineer with whom she had three children, Renee worked part time for a while, then full time as of 1975. She earned a doctorate in social welfare and began advising students and teaching courses on clinical social work practice, specializing in gerontology. She was recognized as one of the School of Social Work's outstanding professors. Later, personal tragedy struck: her husband dropped dead on a tennis court at age fifty-four and she became the family's sole support.

Soon thereafter, Renee decided to supplement her Columbia income by training and developing a private practice as a Gestalt therapist. Seven years ago, with a small private practice and consulting work with social service agencies, staff training workshops on services to the elderly, and supervision of social workers in the field, it was time to step down from Columbia. She did very well. For "Social Work Month" in March 2010 she was honored by St. Barnabas Health Care Network in the Bronx. Her address at the ceremony was about the power of the group and the need for developing social services that empower poor, vulnerable, and oppressed people.

"I always dreamed of making a contribution on a grander scale," she sighs. "I should have joined the Peace Corps so I could travel while being of service. I used to be an activist in the fight for nuclear disarmament, peace, social justice, women's rights, and reproductive freedom, etc., but I was 'chicken.' I guess I was too preoccupied by the need for financial security."

That preoccupation persists today. With the depressed economy, many clients cannot afford to come for therapy even when she lowers her fees. "The insurance companies are killing people and my practice!" she laments. That is not her only worry—her children are in tough shape financially. Renee is contributing support for their health insurance and pays tuition for a grown son who lost his job and is in a retraining program.

Financial pressures are not the only reason Renee will not retire. She cites personal and professional reasons, too. "If I did not have the practice and consultations, I would lose my mind. And I am good at and enjoy what I do!" She is glad to know she is making a contribution. "My legacy is my students who are social workers and deans of graduate schools of social work. They are making the world a better place, and I am proud of them."

Since Renee's family is spread out, she does not see as much of them as she would like. The Jewish holidays are celebrated with many dear friends. In her spare time Renee is active in a lifelong learning community, participates in professional training groups, and enjoys trips with an English hiking group. She has been to England's Lake District, France, Italy, Nepal, and is soon going to Israel. Her health is good, though at seventy-nine she does not have the energy to go nonstop all day and write papers at night, and cannot "hop out of the car like I used to!" Otherwise, she does not feel "old." It's just that with her white hair and wrinkles (they run in the family) people assume she is older than her friends who are actually older than she is.

"Ageism is more subtle than sexism," she finds. "When I walk down the street, nobody notices me any more, and I like to be noticed." She used to refuse when people offered her a seat on the subway. Now she accepts it with good grace. "In the field and at meetings where I am known, I am listened to because of my credibility. I do not know if that would be true if I was not known and people only saw me as an old person."

Renee concedes that it is hard to get older; one has to work at it perhaps more than the other phases of life. Having friends is important, especially younger ones "because the exchange between young and old is vital." Many of her younger friends are still working, and some friends, even younger ones, are frail or have died. She had a significant other for many years who passed away three years ago. Yet aging may be a tougher challenge because people stereotype older adults. "It is a combination of age and gender. A woman has to fight for her place when she is aging. Men have it easier in terms of maintaining their 'place' in society, but then they die earlier. Women typically have better health and live longer. They want to be recognized, to count, too."

Close cousin to the settlement house concept that started Renee Solomon on her career path is the contemporary full-service community school model. Community schools, populated by children and youth considered at risk, remain open for extended hours year round, offering families and community members a menu of health, dental, and social services and recreational and enrichment activities that are provided on site by community agencies. Joy Dryfoos, now eighty-five, is a leader in the community school movement. She is an independent consultant and self-employed researcher who has written about and advocated for full-service community schools for many years. Despite the onset of Parkinson's disease, she is still actively following the growth of the movement, for she feels strongly that one key to graceful aging is maintaining a strong interest in a cause. She advises, "Never retire."

Echoing this advice is another hard-charging and self-employed woman in her seventies, Ann Kaganoff, who asks, "Why retire when you are at the top of your game?" She is working harder than ever, not only to meet her weighty financial obligations, but also because problem solving on behalf of her young clients keeps her sharp. "I never expected to be this busy, this happy, or this good at what I do at my age," she declares.

PROFILE: ANN KAGANOFF

A board-certified educational therapist with a PhD in reading and language development, Ann Kaganoff half-jokingly calls herself the "Resident Granny." In her full-time private practice in Orange County, California, she sees students from elementary school to graduate school, consulting about, assessing, and treating their struggles with a wide range of learning disabilities and other learning challenges. The intervention plans she designs are always individualized and interactive. Ann knows she has credibility: "When I am called into meetings to discuss an individualized education program for a student with special needs, it helps that my title is Doctor, my hair is white, and my experience is so extensive."

"My profession requires me to be problem solving every minute. It keeps me sharp," Ann explains. "In my field, the older you are the better (and I am almost seventy-four), plus having autonomy is a major factor in longevity. I am working harder than I ever have. I never expected to be this busy, this happy, or this good at what I do at my age. I do not intend to retire for at least two more years. Seriously, why retire when you are at the top of your game? Of course it helps to have plenty of clients and rewarding work!"

If she retired, she would garden more, read more, walk more, and write more. She has loads of materials from her staff development workshops for teachers, enough to write a book, for example, on decision making in educational therapy. In addition, her daughters are encouraging her to move closer to them and her grandchildren in Los Angeles, which happens to be a "hotbed" of educational therapy professionals. Those are enticements, and she will move there at some point, but not for a while. Her clients need her too much.

Families in affluent Orange County either have not experienced economic distress during the recession or are sacrificing to ensure that their kids get therapy. In any case, Ann feels extremely fortunate that she has lost few clients in the recession. It could be because, with a quarter century of experience, she is considered a "go-to" person, one of the top educational therapists in Orange County. It could be that families stay with her because it is hard to get on her list. Some families, she calls them the "lifers," stay with her for six or seven years, allowing her to follow many of her clients through important stages of their development. "I always enjoy the kids. They make me laugh. I am at the point in my career where I can be a bit choosy and take the clients I can have a good relationship with and can help."

She and her working friends "are all in the same boat—going on and on and on together. We are all good listeners and love what we do. We work for a variety of reasons; it is not optional for many of us." Ann's own life situation changed some years ago when a divorce caused her income to drop by half, left her carrying a big mortgage, and made financial security more important. In addition, she has a younger sister, born blind, for whom she is now fully responsible. Thus, even if her mortgage was paid off, Ann would still keep working. She cannot think of anything more interesting. Ann likes to say that she is defined by her work and proud of it. "I am glad to be self-sufficient." Thanks to a recent hip replacement surgery, she is healthy and energetic. "I can go at a pretty fast pace for a while longer. I have no plans to quit."

Ann started out as a classroom teacher some fifty-two years ago. Her dad told her she ought to be a teacher so she could take care of herself, and she followed his advice. Later, while pursuing a doctorate in reading and language development at University of California/Santa Barbara, she acquired valuable clinical experience that she deftly parlayed into a faculty position at the University of California/Irvine. As a K–8 literacy specialist directing a reading clinic at the university, she began to pick up private clients. Soon she found her real "home" when she joined the Association of Educational Therapists (AET). She took early retirement from the university and went into private practice full time.

The national professional AET was founded in Southern California and expanded to Northern California, where there is a "big constellation" of educational therapists, as well as to Chicago. The association is not yet quite as well known on the East Coast. A former AET president, Ann would like the membership to reach and serve more kids in public schools where the need is greatest. She has recruited general and special educators to the field, but finds there are not enough training programs targeted to experienced educators. She would like to participate in developing and institutionalizing such programs. Another idea she is mulling over is offering pro bono services to kids who need the therapy but cannot afford it, or meeting them at school or other central locations so that lack of transportation is not an obstacle.

The most exciting new development in Ann's career is mentoring a young educational therapy protégée with whom she meets three times a week for consultation and conversation that is mutually stimulating. They have teamed up to help a child with Fragile X syndrome, a genetic condition causing mental impairment, whom her protégée is tutoring. They also discuss ethical issues and how to set up a private practice. Ann's dream? "If we join forces, with my knowledge of the field and her energy we might start an educational therapy center where kids could be served and professionals trained."

Job status for the older women in my study varies with age and type of work. Just under half of the women are working for an employer. Well over one-third are self-employed, and another 15 percent describe themselves as consultants. There are slightly more full-timers (53 percent) than part-timers (47 percent), regardless of age. Nevertheless, age definitely plays a part in employment decisions. Part-time work is generally favored by women seventy and older (58 percent of women seventy or older are working part time compared to 42 percent working full time), whereas women sixty to sixty-nine tend to choose full-time work (56 percent compared to 44 percent). For women sixty to sixty-nine at least, these survey findings track closely with US BLS national data showing a preference for full-time work among the under seventy-year-olds (see chapter 4).[8]

With support on the rise for telecommuting (working outside the office), with the availability of technologies that make it possible, and with the growing acceptance of so-called flextime (setting one's own work hours within company-defined limits), more employees of all ages in the United States are commuting less, enjoying better work-life balance, while performing their jobs satisfactorily. When such flexibility is company policy, it is sometimes referred to as a results-only work environment, or ROWE. In some organizations full-time employees can compress the work week, that is, work longer hours on some days in exchange for shorter days or a day off during the same pay period.[9] Job sharing, yet another option, has been around for years but is far less prevalent than either telecommuting or flextime.

Companies in the United States are not alone in investing in their human capital in these ways. Owing to the recent contagion of budget deficits, European Union countries too are raising their retirement age and scrambling to find and keep well-qualified employees. Declining birth rates, aging baby boomers, and other demographic developments in Germany, for instance, will result in a shortage of more than three million qualified workers by 2016. As a result, German automakers and other firms have begun making the kinds of targeted adjustments that can benefit older employees and induce them to remain on the job.

Even without a formal ROWE policy to emphasize productivity, a sixty-six-year-old realtor in my study successfully balances her full-time work schedule and family needs: "I do like the flexibility of my work, as I am able to help out with my two grandchildren when my daughter needs me. I do not have a set schedule for seeing them, but rather I am there for the family when asked, if at all possible."

On average, survey respondents have been working for 16.3 years in the current job (or, fifteen median years in the current job). The number of years in the current job ranges widely from three months to fifty years, largely reflecting career changes or getting a "late start" due to time-outs for child rearing in the past, and, possibly, cutbacks or fiscal exigencies associated with the economy today. As is to be expected, the average number of years in the current job is higher among women working full time—eighteen years for full-timers compared to the 16.3 average for all the women collectively. Returning belatedly to the work world is a sixty-two-year-old part-time nurse who raised six children and suddenly finds herself in a difficult situation: "This bad economy has forced me to renew my nursing license and start a new career (something I did not think possible). I try to see it as a new adventure, not just necessity." Adventure? Necessity? In the next chapter we will explore more of the reasons older women give for returning to or remaining in the labor market.

7

Why Older Women Work

Women of the baby boom are expected to spend nearly *three quarters of their adult lives* in the labor force.—Gail Sheehy, Preface to *Women on the Front Lines: Meeting the Challenge of an Aging America*

Older professional women cite myriad reasons for their persistence in the labor force when leisure and retirement beckon. As we shall see, even when they are generally well off, they can be working for financial reasons, such as maintaining health benefits; because they enjoy their work and feel productive; and/or because they fear boredom and an atrophied intellect if they stop. These are the most familiar explanations for delaying retirement cited by the women I surveyed, and they are not dissimilar from recent findings of organizations such as AARP, MetLife, the Employee Benefit Research Institute, and the Pew Research Center. Surveys by these organizations also have found that older women and men across all income groups keep working for a paycheck both because they want to *and* because they need the money for basic expenses, including health insurance, and to live well. However, their survey findings suggest some key differences by race: older African Americans and Hispanic adults are more likely to cite the need for money as their top reason than are whites; and older Hispanic adults are more likely to be supporting other family members than are African Americans and whites.

There can also be more subtle reasons for staying on the job. For example, often mentors and role models have played an important part in women's career decision making, not only in terms of career *choice* but also with respect to the *length* of a career. Sociologist Charles V. Willie draws a useful distinction between mentors and role models: a mentor serves as an advocate whereas a role model is one whose behavior is imitated. For a "cross-gender parental effect" on the education, ambition, and achievement of offspring, Willie says, fathers can mentor highly successful daughters and mothers can influence highly successful sons.[1] His examples include an entrepreneurial father who "passed a torch" of public service to his daughter that she never let go out and fathers who "gave their daughters a sense of security that enabled them to succeed because they were not afraid to risk failure."[2]

The notion of cross-gender parental effect explains a lot about the forty-nine-year career (so far) of the most successful high school basketball coach in the entire country, seventy-three-year-old Leta Andrews, the tough yet respected coach of the Granbury, Texas, high school girls' basketball team. Andrews credits her father for influencing her no-nonsense approach to coaching—he shared his passion for sports and for education with his children, and he also insisted that they perform their farm chores to his exacting standards. I learned about Coach Andrews and her record of 1,346 wins from a front page article in the sports section of the February 15, 2011 *New York Times* (alas, my survey did not get to her).[3] As a varsity basketball player in high school and college, and as a (metaphorical) cheerleader for older women who remain in the workforce, I was delighted to read that this highly competitive woman has no intention of retiring any time soon.

The cross-gender parental effect was also in play in an entirely different milieu as illustrated in the story of business owner Esther Novak, one of my survey respondents. Esther was lucky to have an entrepreneurial father who, as both mentor and role model, encouraged her to be independent and ambitious. Those qualities have helped her manage her consulting, marketing, and communications firm skillfully during the recession.

PROFILE: ESTHER NOVAK

Esther Novak learned to be independent at a fairly early age. Born in Peru, she lost her mother when she was four. A few years later, she and her father came to the United States. English was her second language.

Esther was eager to be interviewed. "Oh, great! Somebody wants to know about my unconventional experience? I love it! I am totally delighted! Our generation was and is pioneering, but we are not recognized at all. I was the only mom in my neighborhood who worked when my kids were in elementary school. My business is about demographics and cultural background, and I find that older career women barely exist in the media."

In 1995 Esther founded a full-service strategic consulting, marketing, and communications firm serving corporations and nonprofit organizations. The agency specializes in multicultural and niche markets. Since the recession, CEO Novak has been redefining the business model to "spread her wings internationally" and to do more cause marketing. She is repositioning her agency using a "Blue Ocean Strategy," W. Chan Kim and Renee Mauborgne's term for finding uncontested market space, a niche that is ready for growth, and where the competition is irrelevant.[4]

Her goals? "That is simple. We are going to recover from the economic downturn and return the business to its previous level of financial success. As for me personally, it would be spending more time with my children and grandchildren, not getting so tired, and having fun outside of work, maybe seeing more of the world—there is more to life!"

Esther expects to continue working "until they put me under!" She has no desire to retire as long as she has her health. She is not afraid of retiring, just has no desire to. "My biggest fear in life is boredom," she confesses.

Esther is a career-changer. During the Carter administration, she directed the National Endowment for the Arts Interdisciplinary Arts Program that provided federal funding for performing arts centers, cultural trade organizations, and leading edge interdisciplinary arts programs. Then she began a career at AT&T where she helped create the AT&T Foundation and led its arts and culture programs nationally. Next, she developed and directed the company's multicultural public relations initiative. "AT&T was an unbelievable training ground. I took some management and marketing classes, learned a lot on the job, and had opportunities to try new things." When the last college tuition bill for her sons was paid, she decided it was time to leave the corporate world and risk a new venture. She modeled the agency on what experience told her was ideal for clients, "the agency I wished I had had when I was the client."

After some thirty-five years in the workforce and at the peak of her career, her reasons for working so hard start with financial realities. Just as the firm was rolling along robustly, the recession hit and caused some clients to pull back for various reasons. "The recession made everything that much harder," she observes ruefully. "It is getting better now, just not fast enough." In addition to practicalities, Esther enjoys using her considerable abilities, gets satisfaction from her work, especially helping others, and enjoys both clients and colleagues.

She describes herself as "very independent." She does not look to friends or family for support regarding her decision to work longer. She sees old friends only occasionally. Many have retired, and several of them do not completely understand why she continues working. Her children give her a hard time about working so hard, urging her to slow down and enjoy life more. Her husband is now her business partner and enjoying it. She insists that her retirement decision has nothing to do with his.

Esther learned to be independent and ambitious from her father, a Peruvian importer-exporter. Although he died when she was in her early twenties, he had definitely impressed his entrepreneurial values on her. She is now expanding her business to the country of her birth. Another role model was a senior administrator at the National Endowment for the Arts, a very ambitious professional woman who raised a son, and later went on to a successful career in commercial real estate. Mindful of the mentoring she benefited from, Esther enjoys advising younger employees in her agency. The people who have worked in her firm have been very loyal and are grateful for her taking their development seriously. She even has reunions with them.

The most gratifying aspects of her work and what she is proudest of are the causes she supports, such as the recognition and respect for people from many different cultures who deserve to be treated fairly. She harnesses the power of the marketplace and the community to recognize and value people for what they are. "I am driven by making a difference," she asserts.

Thus motivated, she has served on nonprofit and major trade association boards, such as the advisory board of El Museo del Barrio in New York City. Honors and awards continue to come her way. For example, she was recognized as Best Businessperson of the Year in the Professional Services category by the Statewide Hispanic Chamber of Commerce of New Jersey and Entrepreneur of the Year by the national *LATINA Style* magazine. She is still learning, too. "I go to professional conferences. I grab whatever learning will serve me in the work I do."

Now in her sixties, she muses, "I am more conscious of time going by and not having as much energy. It bothers the hell out of me. I do not look my age and do not feel my age, but my body knows. Fortunately, I enjoy good health and I am as productive at work as ever." She would be quick to advise other older women to continue working as long as they wish. "Why not?" she shrugs. "Do not let anyone talk you out of it. Age is just a number. Interest and energy are what count."

A hard-working father was an early inspiration and guide for another woman, now a travel agent in her seventies, who recalls working in her father's drug store when she was young. "It was the best training I ever had," she says. Then again, a parent may be a *negative* role model, someone a young person hopes never to emulate. A few high-achieving women told me they knew early on that they most definitely did *not* want to be like their mothers. One businesswoman said that she was determined to have a career other than homemaking, the only available path where and when she grew up. A librarian said that education and a career were ways of avoiding her mother's situation—financial dependence on her husband, powerlessness, and lack of choices.

The influences on Gayle Rich's career moves were uniformly positive. The people who inspired Gayle as she built her career in arts administration were Rudolf Serkin, John Cage, and John Langstaff. As you will learn from her profile, she quickly came to admire these three highly creative musicians not only for their stellar accomplishments but also for the passion that drove their work. More recently, as she herself has gotten older, Gayle is finding a positive role model in her bright and active ninety-six-year-old mother.

PROFILE: GAYLE RICH
Gayle Rich, longtime executive director of Revels, Inc., found her niche in arts management by accident. "There was no grand plan. I just rolled from one thing to the next, producing concerts, bringing people to hear music, doing what I enjoyed and what was important to me," she said. After college at the

University of Kansas and at Oberlin in the early 1960s, Gayle started out as
a registered music therapist. She moved on to social work, which she loved
but found tremendously demanding. Social work was no longer a good fit
when she became a divorced single mom with two young kids. She considered
enrolling in an arts administration program at Harvard but was advised that
she might learn equally well what she needed to know by volunteering for a
few Boston-area arts organizations. Most people would have understood this
advice to mean serving just one organization at a time. Gayle took it to mean
volunteering at three places in tandem. Since she was an accomplished violist,
working with the musical instrument collection at the Museum of Fine Arts
in Boston was a good place to start her apprenticeship.

Soon she had landed a summer job for world-renowned pianist Rudolf
Serkin, working with the summer concerts at Marlboro Music, which Serkin
cofounded. He hired her not because of her musical abilities but because of
her social work background—her ability to listen to temperamental artists! As
she was organizing concerts at the Old South Meeting House, at the Institute
of Contemporary Art in Boston, and at the DeCordova Museum in Lincoln,
she had figured out that the performing arts field was where she belonged.
Like the viola (her instrument of choice) whose role is to support the violin,
Gayle would join a music organization on the "back" side. That is, her interest
lay in helping to shape the artistic vision for the music and in supporting the
performing artists who would be out front.

And then, fortunately, Gayle and the Revels found each other. Revels artistic and music director John Langstaff invited Gayle to produce *The Christmas
Revels for 1977.* In case you have not heard of the Revels, here is a thumbnail
sketch. Revels, Inc., was founded in 1971 by musician, educator, and author
Langstaff and his daughter, Carol, to celebrate world cultures and traditions
through music, dance, storytelling, pagan and older Christian rituals, and,
always, audience participation. Best known is *The Christmas Revels* in Cambridge, Massachusetts, which for forty years has celebrated the return of light
at the winter solstice. Whether the theme for music, drama, and dance in a
given year is medieval, Renaissance, Victorian, Armenian, Russian, or Appala-
chian, audiences are sure to see their perennial favorites performed by Morris
dancers, mummers, bagpipers, and St. George and the Dragon. Oldsters and
youngsters delight in the singing of carols and rounds and then linking hands
with many hundreds of other Revelers as they noisily process around the great

hall of Sanders Theatre singing "Lord of the Dance" to the accompaniment of a symphonic brass ensemble. (I speak from happy experience and fond memory. *The Christmas Revels* was a traditional holiday treat for my family.)

Programming expanded greatly over the years under Gayle's leadership. John Langstaff remained involved until his death in 2005 at age eighty-five. More recent Revels programs, also based on historic, seasonal, and cultural themes, celebrate the autumnal equinox—the River Sing—and the vernal equinox—the Spring Sing. Revels productions are comprised of a volunteer chorus of children and adults as well as professional actors, musicians, designers, and directors. At the center of each Revels are the dancers, singers, and storytellers who present the arts and traditions of the featured cultures.

A commitment to educational programming for children and families is the legacy of Langstaff's rich and varied career as an educator, musicologist, and early music revivalist. (Again I can speak from personal experience: when I was a classroom teacher in the mid-1970s, I took an introductory music course at Boston College that was taught by John Langstaff himself.) A forty-member touring ensemble brings Revels programs to public venues and schools throughout southern New England. In addition to year-round family programming, Revels offers recordings, songbooks, lesson plans, how-to manuals, and choral arrangements of the music from its performances.

Also during Gayle's tenure, the Revels have expanded geographically. There are now production companies in nine other cities besides Cambridge: New York City; Washington, D.C.; Hanover, New Hampshire; Oakland and Santa Barbara, California; Houston, Texas; Tacoma, Washington; Portland, Oregon; and Boulder, Colorado. Gayle has convened annual conferences for the producers and directors from all ten cities. And she has succeeded in getting Revels on solid financial footing.

Back in 1977, however, Gayle did not even have an office; she worked out of her dining room. Time passed, Revels rented office space in a church basement, and in 1984 the board invited her to be the executive director. She agreed to try it for six months ("to see if I would be an effective leader," she explains modestly), and she has stayed for twenty-seven years.

Gayle describes herself as "pretty wired," with lots of energy. "Revels is a huge part of my life," she says. "We grew the organization a while back and took another giant leap five years ago. Although I try to keep my work life and private life separate and even have made rules for myself, such as not checking work-related e-mails from home at night, Revels is very much a multitask operation that takes a huge amount of time. However, all told, I would have to say that my family always comes first."

When I asked Gayle who had inspired her along the way, she mentioned Rudolf Serkin, John Cage, and John Langstaff because they all loved their work and were driven by it, yet they all had fun doing it. Gayle also mentioned Charlotte, her ninety-six-year-old mother, who exercises, reads three books a week, and "is focused, lucid, and interested in things." Gayle moved her mother three years ago from California, where she had lived her entire life, to Cambridge. When Gayle was a child, Charlotte worked from home as a public stenographer, typing papers for doctors and dentists and graduate students. "The difference between your work and mine," Charlotte has told Gayle, "is that you love what you do and I was just trying to make ends meet."

Gayle thinks of her ninety-six-year-old mother as old, certainly not herself, merely sixty-nine albeit a grandmother. Recently, however, she saw a different picture of herself through another person's eyes when she happened to be seated on a plane beside a young teenage girl with whom she chatted pleasantly. When the passengers disembarked, the teen's father was waiting and asked his daughter how the trip had been. Gayle was shocked to overhear her tell her father that it was fine because she was sitting next to "a nice old lady."

Nonetheless, age awareness is by no means what spurred Gayle to plan her retirement. It was more a matter of believing that organizations grow and change with the times. Calculating how many years she had been at Revels got her thinking along new lines, and she quietly began setting retirement decision goals. On the one hand, she knew she would miss the wonderful community of Revels friends—audiences, producers, directors, and performers—she had made in Cambridge and during visits to the other Revels sites. On the other, she admitted to herself that she was not bouncing back so easily from the cross-country trips. She realized that she had been dragging her feet about painting and other time-consuming home projects. When she noticed that many of her friends were moving to part-time work, she wondered whether she too could do that. If she could cut back to, say, three days a week, she would have more time for grandchildren, gardening, and the other things she is passionate about. However, once the Great Recession struck, she realized that she needed to work longer not less. During the most difficult months of the recession, the

Revels organization instituted tough cost-saving measures—her entire staff took a two-week furlough, there were no raises, and the staff had to contribute to medical insurance costs for the first time.

Gayle finally decided that she would tie her retirement to a very important event. The fortieth anniversary of the Revels would be an optimal time to step aside. When during a Revels dinner for board and staff she announced her decision to retire, many were surprised yet understanding. Her colleagues are planning a "Gayla" gala and fundraiser to celebrate forty years of Revels, honor Gayle's twenty-seven years at the helm of the organization, and welcome her replacement, the longtime executive director of the Boston Gay Men's Chorus, who Gayle describes as "a fabulous choice."

Upon retirement, Gayle intends to take six months to step back, explore, and figure out her next phase. She will take a string quintet to Jamaica as she has done every year. She will take a trip with a friend to Prague, Vienna, and Budapest. She and her viola will join the Manhattan String Quartet for a week of study. She anticipates difficult moments with absolutely nothing to do, but is looking forward to seeing what that is like.

Businesswoman Esther Novak and arts administrator Gayle Rich are but two of the many women (over three-quarters of the survey respondents) who could cite one or more mentors and role models. People who had positively influenced respondents' careers included:

Mother, father, or both parents: forty-three mentions (37 percent)

Colleagues (female): thirty-one mentions (27 percent)

Boss, supervisor, employer: twenty-five mentions (22 percent)

Professor, dean, advisor, college president: twenty-two mentions (19 percent)

Friends: seventeen mentions (15 percent)

Teacher, counselor: seventeen mentions (15 percent)

Husband, significant other, partner, boyfriend: fifteen mentions (13 percent)

Note: This list includes multiple mentions.

Other strong influences on career choice and duration came from unspecified family members, children, grandparents, aunt, uncle, religious figures, the women's movement in the 1960s and 1970s, and assorted famous figures, including the intrepid girl detective Nancy Drew! A minister told me that she discovered the world of books thanks to her "pseudo-grandparents" and thanks to a high school history teacher who challenged her academically. She also remembers a male Unitarian-Universalist minister who served as a fine role model at a time when there were few female ministers.

Respondents say they enjoy mentoring their younger colleagues and new hires. Having been guided along the way by their predecessors, they receive great satisfaction nurturing fledgling careers, teaching the "ropes," and giving back to the field. As we have seen in chapter 6, the young Renee Solomon found her calling early on when social workers at the neighborhood settlement house took her under their collective wing. Many of the baby boomers who are joining the ranks of older professionals have had the benefit of mentoring, and many of them are passing along what they have learned to the generations following them. This is true of attorney Arden Lang whose parents were her earliest role models. Now the oldest person working in her agency, she makes a point of mentoring new hires. So long as she enjoys defending clients and coaching other lawyers, she will continue to work.

PROFILE: ARDEN LANG

Attorney Arden Lang believes that humans make a difference in improving the lives of ordinary people. She has always wanted to help others. "My job is to help the most despised people in our society—convicted, incarcerated felons. It is emotionally draining, but it needs to be done. My colleagues and I share a passion for this work."

She has been with the Office of the State Appellate Defender in Illinois for twenty-five years, first as Assistant Appellate Defender and now as a supervisor. Anyone convicted of a felony in Illinois is entitled to one appeal, represented by private counsel or by her office. Arden spends half her time writing appellate briefs and arguing in appellate court, state Supreme Court, or federal court, and the other half supervising lawyers in her office as they produce appellate briefs and prepare for oral argument.

Arden's dad was an attorney who often told stories about his work and encouraged her to become a lawyer. He saw that she was interested in the law from an early age. "Do something useful when you grow up," he urged. "Why would you want to spend your time washing someone's socks?" Arden had other role models as well: her mother, a trained social worker during the Depression, and her paternal grandmother, who owned a millinery shop and worked into her late seventies, even when the fashion was to go hatless and business was slow. "She had an immigrant's drive toward self-improvement," Arden recounts. "This amazing woman got up very early and took her golf clubs on the streetcar to play nine holes before work. She cooked meals for her family in a little kitchen set up in the back of her shop."

When her father died in 1977, Arden had spent six years teaching grade school in Chicago, had two children, and was going through a divorce. Her brother then assumed the role of reminding her of her career goal. She took up the challenge, attended Northwestern University, and earned a JD. She remarried (to an attorney) and led a life well balanced between family and work. "I did not have to sacrifice one for the other. I attended my kids' plays and teacher conferences. I could park a sick child in my office if I needed to. I was not beset with a working mother's guilt." Today, there is no question that family, which now includes grandchildren, is number one. Her ninety-six-year-old mother lives with her.

In addition to balancing work and family for thirty-seven years, Arden has always pursued volunteer activities. Going forward, she thinks she should do more intensive work for fewer organizations. She serves on the board of a women's shelter, has mentored a troubled girl in the Big Brother/Big Sister program for five years, and engages in political campaigns, most recently in support of Barack Obama's election. And in her leisure time it is yoga that she enjoys.

Although half of her dearest friends have retired, she and her husband have no plans to stop working. They will make their decisions independently. "When a person gets to the point where she sits at work regretting being there, it is time to leave." In her opinion, women should work at something productive, so long as they can afford to do that, so long as they have a choice. It has not escaped her notice that younger people in her office are starting to retire; at sixty-seven she has become the oldest person in the agency. "I used to say I would retire in three years, then it was another three years, and it keeps pushing ahead. I will retire only when my job becomes too difficult or too tiring or no longer interesting or when I lose pride in helping my clients and other lawyers."

Arden does occasionally wonder what the future will hold. Reading, exercise, vacations and visits with family come readily to mind. Longer term, she knows she has financial security. While she and her husband do not earn huge salaries, they have both worked in government jobs for many years and have government pensions. (Although the state is in terrible shape because of the recession and next year's budget is a big worry, government pensions are constitutionally guaranteed in Illinois.) More immediately, tremendous changes are afoot in her work environment. When the people who started the agency retired, the agency grew exponentially and became almost completely paperless. Work is now done online—research, preparation of briefs, information storage, and so on. Technology has made everyone far more efficient; the pace is positively frenetic. However, technology has driven out the "family feeling" that came with collegial relationships, and the old environment is missed even though she embraces the new era. Arden has no problems with technology and can even out-produce new, inexperienced attorneys. "I do not have to spin my wheels as much as they do and know how to manage my time more effectively. I enjoy mentoring the new hires."

Compared with the rampant discrimination female attorneys often faced in earlier generations when they were offered secretarial jobs instead of the legal work for which they were trained, Arden has had no problems with discrimination. By the time she went to Northwestern, 40 percent of her law school class was female (and it is even higher today). When female lawyers in Illinois disdained the "smokers" where their male counterparts congregated and networked, they formed their own bar association. Today, she finds that she and her appellate defender colleagues have more in common than not, even though most of them have young families. "We share a vision with respect to our work." The only place where she perceives a cultural divide and feels like a dinosaur is at "trivia contests," which are very popular in Springfield. She is part of a crack trivia team that does really well. "But our expertise is too nineteenth century," she groans. "We need to recruit younger players who can handle the pop culture questions."

Arden thinks women become "invisible" as they age. "Sixty may be the dividing line. Yet it is a liberating experience, a woman is freer to say what she believes, so long as she doesn't bore people by droning on about what used to be!"

The longest-serving professional woman I interviewed takes mentoring very seriously. Dr. Dollye M. E. Robinson is dean of the School of Liberal Arts and Professor of Music at Jackson State University in Mississippi. Helping students to develop as people and to become proficient in their fields, being a role model for the students, faculty, and staff under one's care—these constitute the true purpose of higher education, she believes. And the numerous band teachers and orchestra leaders whom she taught and has mentored over the years attest to her high standards. She intends to continue working as long as the university needs her, and as long as she is doing something valuable that enables others to grow *and* herself to grow.

PROFILE: DOLLYE M. E. ROBINSON

"I do not count the years, so I will not tell you my age." So began this interviewer's conversation with the formidable Dr. Dollye M. E. Robinson, who has worked at Jackson State University (JSU) in Mississippi's capital in one capacity or another for nearly sixty years. As dean of the College of Liberal Arts and Professor of Music, Dollye not only oversees the largest college at JSU (there are ten departments), she also teaches a course in music history that meets at 8:00 a.m., three times a week. She is at the peak of her career and then some. She has not given any thought to retirement; she declares that she will continue as long as she is able. "You could say that I am married to my profession. I am very active and thoroughly enjoy what I'm doing."

In Dollye's view, the primary purpose of higher education is helping students develop as people and become proficient in their fields. "Younger people are learning from me. Being a role model makes you stay on your toes so you do a better job for the students, faculty, and staff under your care. As an educated woman who educates others, I believe in spreading my knowledge and encouraging them to do the right thing at the university. I feel I am needed."

JSU calls itself the Urban University of the State of Mississippi. Founded in 1877 as Jackson College, it later was called Jackson State College and by 1974 had become the large public, coeducational university it is today. According to Carnegie Classification, JSU is one of three historically black doctoral/research universities.

One of Dollye's proudest achievements was getting Jackson College accredited regionally and nationally in the early days. The president appointed her as chair of the self-study committee that was successful in gaining recognition by the Southern Association of Colleges and Schools and the National Association of Schools of Music.

A true Jacksonian, Dollye was raised in Jackson and still lives in the house in which she was born, which happens to be one block away from the university. Encouraged by her mother and by her teachers, she excelled as the only female trumpet player in her high school jazz band. This distinction won her a scholarship to Jackson College, where she remembers playing whichever band instrument was needed. After graduating in 1948, her first job was music teacher and band director at Alexander High School in Brookhaven, Mississippi. In 1952 she returned to Jackson College as assistant band director and instructor of music. As the band flourished (it became the "Sonic Boom of the South") and her career took off, she was appointed to positions of increasing responsibility—in a unanimous vote, by the faculty of the Music Department, she became head of the Music Department. Subsequently, she was made chair of the Division of Fine Arts, then became assistant dean, associate dean, and was appointed to dean of the School of Liberal Arts. Along the way, in the 1950s (she is deliberately vague about the dates) she earned two master's degrees and a PhD in music and administration from Northwestern University.

Dollye has mentored numerous students over the years, instilling them with what experience has taught her about life, learning, and people. Her former students are spread out all across the country as band teachers and orchestra leaders. Years ago she took under her wing a scholarship student who became an outstanding band director. This student has since retired to pursue writing interests, and now, in a mutually beneficial turnabout, looks out for her.

The "Senior Dean" (a nickname she does not mind at all) is obviously held in high regard. Fellow JSU administrators look after her, escorting her to committee meetings, and making sure that she is comfortably seated. In 1998 the Dollye M. E. Robinson Endowed Scholarship Fund was established. Soon, Dollye, together with Dr. James E. Lyons, Sr. (then president of JSU), was providing significant input in the design of a new building that was dedicated and named the Dollye M. E. Robinson School of Liberal Arts Building in 2001.

A member of numerous professional organizations over the years, Dollye is particularly active on the Mississippi Humanities Council and the Mississippi Arts Commission. She is also a life member of Alpha Kappa Alpha, the national Greek-letter sorority established by black college women at Howard University in 1908 to provide community service programs. Dollye embodies the sorority's ideals: an unwavering quest for excellence and exemplary role modeling; motivation to outstanding achievements; encouragement toward individual growth; sincere fellowship, loyalty, faith, and unity.

Dollye says that she doesn't act or feel old. She thinks only in terms of personal growth and helping others, not the number of years that have passed. In the midst of the current economic stagnation, her greatest concern has been finding financial support for needy students whose Pell grants do not go far enough. She is not concerned about her own financial well-being as she says that she has always had enough to take care of herself and provide for others, as well. "I live peacefully and happily with what I have and galvanize my resources to help others, not only financially but also educationally and personally."

Good health and fitness are other important keys to her success. "Students expect you to look and act well. You have to be able to move at a fast pace; you can't drag around with your head hanging low, and you have to have a smile on your face."

Here is her advice to women considering working past retirement age: "First, make sure you are capable of doing your job well. Do you have a 'good head'? Can you deal with people and help to move them forward? Second, don't just do it for the money. Third, do something valuable that enables others to grow *and* yourself to grow. And fourth, evaluate yourself regularly: if you are not producing anything valuable, then stop!"

After imparting these words of wisdom, Dollye went on to say that she appreciates my efforts to present older women who are still on the job. In her opinion, the book "will be shared all around the country and will encourage professional women like myself to continue doing our important work."

Older career women like Arden and Dollye and the others whom I interviewed express the pride and satisfaction they feel in a job exceedingly well done. When asked for their reasons for staying on the job, regardless of the field in which they are employed they typically say it is because they know they are making a difference. And, tellingly, for each of these women, working in the senior years is largely a matter of *choice.*

In contrast, many men and women, regardless of age, are forced to stay with a job simply because they need the income and depend on the benefits. Health insurance at least partially paid by one's employer is particularly prized. Even with Medicare, maintaining adequate health insurance coverage through one's senior years can be challenging, particularly after retirement. Fortunately, most of my respondents are healthy; in fact, relatively few of the women (14 percent) are troubled by physical ailments or limitations of any kind.

One half of the survey respondents are receiving benefits from their current employer who contributes to some or most of the following (in descending order of frequency)—vacation days, health insurance, retirement savings plan, sick leave, disability insurance, life insurance, pension. When there are no job benefits from a current employer, it is usually because they are part-timers or self-employed or they are collecting benefits from a previous employer. A few rely on their husband's benefits or purchase benefits for themselves. A sixty-six-year-old fundraising consultant self-provides: "I am nice to me—that's it!"

That "pension" falls in last place among benefits enumerated on the survey is consistent with the trend reported by the US BLS and discussed in chapter 4: fewer companies are committing to pay workers a set amount in retirement benefits. Thus, as the savings burden shifts away from employers, workers' pension income will likely become a thing of the past.

Other benefits contributed by some employers include: dental insurance, a free meal in the employee cafeteria, a museum pass, and tuition for continuing education. The American woman who is teaching school in Senegal—you will read her story in chapter 8—is pleased to have her housing and utilities paid for, airfare to the United States, and a shipping allowance.

Just as women give a variety of reasons for staying on the job, some reasons clearly recession-related and some not, the alternatives—reducing their hours or retiring completely—mean different things to different people. One full-time university faculty developer who has turned sixty admits: "I am somewhat scared of retirement, even though I am not a big spender. No income? Oh my! I hope to work to age sixty-seven at least." Some cannot wait for it, some dread it, and some comfort themselves by saying they are "semi-retired." I was in that camp, though I gradually dropped the "semi." The dear man I have been married to for nearly fifty years is a professor who continues to teach and do research mainly because he loves his work and also because we want our retirement savings to grow. Then again, he has another reason for putting off *emeritus* status: "When I am home all the time," he predicts, "we will be constantly bumping into each other in the kitchen!"

Here is the perspective on retirement of another sixty-year-old, a full-time director of oncology services:

In 2005, when I was fifty-five, I found myself "between opportunities" for nine months. I had sold a small business and could have chosen to retire at that time but found that when people asked me about how my retirement was, I was *really* uncomfortable and I chose to say that I was "on sabbatical." I was delighted when another opportunity presented itself. Even though I was incredibly busy with volunteer activities and hiking and biking, I was bored and felt that my life, without work, lacked form and substance. Just a year ago, I accepted a new administrative position and love the work and the organization I work for. It is a fairly low-stress job in spite of the fact that I have a lot of responsibility. Being off for nine months caused me to set my sights on retirement at age sixty-five or sixty-six. My husband is ten years older and has no desire to retire. We have saved so that we could retire now but just do not want to be out of the workforce. Our parents are deceased and our children are grown. We do take about seven weeks of vacation each year and have traveled extensively. I would, however, love to have more time with our grandchildren. Only two of the six live in this area. I clearly am choosing to work past the age of sixty, and my husband is doing the same (past seventy). We both enjoy great health and retirement is not really all that appealing.

Aside from the universal attractions of earning money and accruing job benefits, there are many other compelling arguments for continuing to work. A sixty-three-year-old speech/language pathologist explains her reasoning this way: "First, it is a joint decision with my husband. We share a vague sense that we are not at the 'retirement' stage of life. Next, it is the tension around contemplating transitions—I have *always* worked. And last but not least, it is pride in doing something people are willing to pay for."

Actually, compared to the hardships and financial uncertainties befalling so many Americans today, even those who do have jobs, the older professional women I studied are relatively well off. More than half (57 percent) indicate candidly that they *need* the income; some simply *like* the income. Less than one-third (30 percent) are working to save more in 401k plans or other retirement plans. Still fewer are trying to boost Social Security benefits as high as possible (28 percent), keep up with rising health insurance costs (21 percent), cope with other financial pressures (16 percent), or accrue pension benefits (15 percent). Here is one woman's honest assessment of her situation: "This is a good time for feeling happy with my track record and looking forward to bigger accomplishments, but a difficult setback in the economy has put a wrench in those efforts—hopefully only temporarily."

An entirely different reason for not retiring comes from Danielle Boal, MD, a sixty-four-year-old professor of radiology and pediatrics: "I enjoy my work, but I am seriously considering part time. I am afraid if I stop completely my mental acuities would diminish and I would accomplish less."

PROFILE: DANIELLE BOAL

Danielle Boal is distinguished professor of Radiology and Pediatrics and chief of Pediatric Radiology at the Penn State Milton S. Hershey Medical Center. The long-awaited freestanding Penn State Children's Hospital is scheduled to open in 2012. She is a fellow of the American College of Radiologists and received the Presidential Award from the Society for Pediatric Radiology.

Early in her career, Danielle trained in a pediatric radiology fellowship program at Children's Hospital in Boston and then went directly to the Hershey Medical Center. When she was first hired at Hershey she headed a department of one. For more than thirty-four years she has built a six-person team.

"The bulk of my time, maybe 70 percent, is devoted to patient care. As chief I am also responsible for administrative work, and I consult and do research on child abuse. Of course, I have radiology residents and medical students with me every day, so I am also a teacher. Teaching medical students and residents to care for patients and monitoring their work is only part of it—it is just as important to inspire them to be ethical physicians." Danielle sets a good example by serving on the State Attorney General's Medical Legal Advisory Board reviewing postmortem x-rays for Pennsylvania coroners and consulting with lawyers and social services on suspected abuse cases. "There are many unknowns in child abuse. Some people do not want to believe it really exists, but it is certainly real and the public is well aware. We do try to take a balanced view to protect the children at risk while avoiding erroneous accusations."

Danielle thinks she is one of the more productive doctors in her division. "It depends on the day," she notes. Her specialty is diagnostic radiology, including radiographs, fluoro ultrasound, and CT. She regrets not becoming proficient in magnetic resonance (MR imaging) when that technology came along. "If I could revisit that decision I would, but in reality I am too busy with day-to-day responsibilities to carve out the big chunk of time required for the training. I look at the imaging and I am comfortable with the anatomy, but I do not formally interpret the studies because of my lack of training/experience."

Danielle, age sixty-four, and her husband Dick, an orthopedic surgeon, have three grown sons. In the past, as the two Drs. Boal threw themselves into their work, they were very lucky to have Dick's Aunt Marge live with the family and look after the boys. "The kitchen was Aunt Marge's turf and that meant I never had to cook!" Danielle recalls. "When she passed away at age ninety-three this past year, Dick and I were living alone for the first time in years."

Danielle plans to continue working but is considering cutting back to half-time status in another year or so to allow for more clinical research and writing. She would like to be able to spend more time with her grandchildren who live in Colorado and improve her physical fitness. She barely has time to walk the dog and muck out the stalls of—let alone ride—the two horses she boards at a nearby stable. There has not been much room for other leisure pursuits or traveling, as she has been pretty much tied down to the hospital.

There are other reasons for not retiring altogether, particularly money issues. For one, Danielle wants to be there for family members who need financial help. For another, she would like to be able to continue making contributions to charitable organizations. Then there is her husband's expensive hobby/passion since medical school—he has just earned a captain's rating and enjoys flying a jet that he co-owns as part of a charter business. He plans to work for several more years and would like her to continue working too.

Of course, cutting back to part time and halving her salary would improve the department's budgetary picture: owing to the recession, the Penn State M. S. Hershey Medical Center has increased financial pressures for the first time. Still, total retirement seems to be out of the question for this intensely focused career woman. "I am ambivalent about cutting back because I know I get more accomplished when I am busy and under pressure. I worry about being lazy if I stay in bed an hour longer than usual. A full slate of gardening, learning to cook, and reading, all of which I enjoy in smaller doses, would not be satisfying. I need deadlines and schedules and people depending on me. At other times, though, I think I have been doing this work long enough!"

A recent study by two economists lends strong support to Danielle's notion regarding potential diminishment of mental alertness if she stopped working. Using comparable data sets from the United States, England, and eleven other European countries, Robert Willis and Susann Rohwedder found that early retirement may impair memory while work helps maintain cognitive functioning in men and women in their sixties. The study did take into consideration the countries' different retirement ages—people typically retire later in the United States, England, and Denmark, where performance on memory tests was highest, and they retire earlier in France, Italy, and Spain, where scores were lowest. And though the economists did not uncover what specific parts of the work experience and aspects of the work environment can contribute to better performance on cognitive tests, their study's conclusions are attracting attention from other researchers and reminding the rest of us to "use it or lose it."[5]

For many of the women I studied, working is synonymous with self-esteem and well-being. A sixty-one-year-old self-employed educational therapist who works full time sees it that way: "I feel very alive when I work and feel much healthier. I was ill briefly and continued to work because it gave me an identity beyond my illness. I cannot imagine retiring but perhaps cutting back in the later years." A sense of well-being can also derive from avoiding the boredom trap. Highly active women do not like to have time on their hands. It may be an old saw, but a job keeps a person busy and gets her out of the house. Quite a few of the women in my study admit to feeling that way (42 percent).

Nearly all are finding their work satisfying and meaningful (91 percent). Their jobs allow them to put their considerable abilities, skills, and professional training to good use (85 percent). A sixty-three-year-old education foundation director admits: "I am not ready to retire yet. I receive pleasure from feeling needed and contributing to my community in an important role." Similarly, Susan Damour, an energetic sixty-six-year-old, recalls how she tried and "flunked" retirement three years ago. Boredom was one problem, the recession was another. Now back at work in an exciting and demanding government job, she oversees the General Services Administration's (GSA) work in the six-state Rocky Mountain region.

PROFILE: SUSAN DAMOUR

Susan Damour tried retirement briefly and did not particularly like it. What she does like is doing deals. She recently came out of retirement to put her community relations skills and political acumen to good use as the regional administrator for GSA, the federal agency that designs, builds, and maintains all the federal buildings, courthouses, and ports of entry across the country. The GSA also provides federal agencies with IT services, automobiles, furniture, office supplies, and equipment to facilitate their missions. As an appointee of the Obama administration, Sue's Rocky Mountain Region encompasses Colorado, Utah, North Dakota, South Dakota, Montana, and Wyoming.

Sue was "incredibly thrilled and incredibly lucky" to return this year to the same position she held during the Clinton administration. "It was sheer fate," she explains modestly. She is dedicated to building environmental awareness, developing renewable energy sources, and reducing the federal carbon footprint. "Droughts and forest fires caused by rising temperatures are taking a terrible toll in the West," she despairs. Also passionate about the arts, she partners with local cultural councils to get the government's art resources out of federal warehouses and into the region.

Her goal is to share the "good, textured experience" she acquired during forty-two years in the workforce so her organization "makes someone's life better every day." She can tap into her network to open doors and help people and communities reach their goals. "Everyone should be able to participate fully in society and have a shot at the American dream," she insists. "I am working with great people, and I love what I am doing!"

In addition to having a type-A personality, where did all Sue's zest for work come from? Her mother taught her the meaning of hard work. "Nobody is going to take care of you," she admonished Sue from an early age. "You will have to do it yourself." Her mother was a costume designer on Broadway and a fabulous cook. Friends insisted she start a catering business, and her mother worked into her eighties. The family lived comfortably in Darien, an affluent Connecticut suburb. In reaction to WASP-y, elitist values common there in the 1950s and 1960s and defined by her generation's affinity for social and political movements—free speech, civil rights, antiwar, and feminism—Sue became an ardent liberal and activist.

Her mother scoffed at feminism even though she herself embodied many of its tenets. "When I declared that I wanted to be a judge, my mother told me I could not because, as a female, I was not going to be a lawyer." So after college, she embarked on a series of poorly paid jobs. She married young, had a child, and was divorced by age thirty. With the wolf lurking at her door, she began selling jewelry and "crab-walked her way to self-sufficiency." She also was determined to support a new effort she believed in called Common Cause, the nonpartisan, nonprofit advocacy organization founded in 1970 by John Gardner to promote political change, government accountability, and citizen participation in democracy. Toting her baby on her back as she canvassed shopping malls, she applied her sales experience to become a highly effective Common Cause recruiter and fundraiser. Before long, she was invited to serve on the Common Cause board. Soon the governor of Colorado hired her to manage the governor's mansion, serve as the executive aide to the governor's wife, and coordinate kids' and women's issues. Eventually, her political skills and personal moxie led to the GSA position for the Clinton administration. When the Bush administration came in, she took a job as a senior vice president at a nonprofit organization. The secret to her success? "I moved up because I took on increased responsibility."

Retirement at age sixty-three seemed sensible when her second husband, who she describes as "adorable," "phenomenal," and "a home run guy," had retired from his legal practice. Soon, their combined income dropped, and, just as troublesome, boredom set in for her. Book clubs, knitting, and creative cooking did not fill the void. The recession only made things worse. "I became more cautious and totally changed my spending habits. Now at sixty-six, I really do not need any more things. With good health and my exciting job, my husband and I will make our shared resources last into old age."

Sue travels away from her home in Denver, puts in long days and often weekends as well, and does not have much vacation time. Still, she has plenty of energy and no stress. "Plus," she points out, "I have a loving family, including a terrific granddaughter, and I live in the most beautiful part of the country." When Sue returned to government work this year, one friend commented that Sue had "flunked retirement and was not cut out for it anyway." Her husband gave her return to work his whole-hearted support. She is now the primary breadwinner as, curiously, are all the females in her extended family.

"We do not look or act like our grandmothers," Sue observes. "We are making valuable contributions in the workforce, so men no longer have to carry the load all by themselves. . . . My clothing is stylish, pretty 'hip,' though age appropriate," she continues. "I think of myself as equal to my younger colleagues. I keep my weight under control. Technology is not a problem. I am not fazed by my laptop or my Blackberry, but I do not blog or do Facebook or Twitter. I can't say I know how to set up "cloud" computing (information technology delivery services based on the Internet), but fortunately I have staff who do!"

Her advice to other women: "If you are passionate about something, go make it happen. Meet a need. Ability is ageless." And with that, Sue is off to work on a big renewable energy deal.

Among the important reasons cited for staying on the job by the women I surveyed is enjoying their clients, patients, students, or customers (80 percent)

as well as the pleasure of helping others, making a contribution, and making a difference (81 percent). A sixty-one-year-old kitchen and bath designer maintains: "I would probably stay working in my field even if money was not needed! It is creative, stimulating, and helpful and I have good communication with a variety of clients." They also say they generally enjoy their colleagues and coworkers, if any (69 percent).

Many men and women have to stop working when they lose their health, no matter how old they are. Fortunately, two-thirds of the women in my study can report that they are enjoying good health and high energy (66 percent). A sixty-six-year-old studio artist asserts: "I feel energized and smart about work. However, nothing is accomplished as quickly as previously—no surprise there!" A few of my respondents are truly exceptional athletes. A California college professor (an old friend with whom I learned to swim at summer camp when we were eight years old) took up ocean swimming years ago and is now a master's-level swimmer and serious triathlete who competes in races from Maine to California and Hawaii. Another good friend in her mid-sixties, whom I profiled in chapter 2, teaches medical language courses, is working on the tenth edition of her best-selling medical terminology textbook, and has run nine marathons to raise money for pediatric cancer and breast cancer research. Without necessarily being as competitive or engaging in as strenuous a training regimen as these two working friends, the women who report good health and high energy all attribute their ability to keep working to first-rate fitness and vigor. Although physical ailments or limitations trouble a small number, they are, nonetheless, all still working.

Less than one-third (30 percent) describe themselves as "at the peak" of their careers. This outcome for women sixty or older after many years in the workforce may be ascribed to starting late after time out for raising a family (as 14 percent did), or to changing the career field one or more times, as nearly one-third did (30 percent). Dr. Margaret Beale Spencer, now the Marshall Field IV Professor of Urban Education in the Comparative Human Development Department at the University of Chicago, first studied to become a registered pharmacist. The following profile sketches the career moves that have brought her to the peak of her profession and describes the substance of her challenging work on behalf of at-risk youth.

PROFILE: MARGARET BEALE SPENCER

Dr. Margaret Beale Spencer is a developmental psychologist, with interests in life span human development. She specializes in youth development with an emphasis on children's development taking place in varying cultural contexts and, concurrently, she explores adolescents' efforts to achieve resiliency and academic success. Her basic research and application collaborations focus on urban youth of all races and ethnicities. An early and consistent focus is the development of black male youth as they transition into young adulthood. Now sixty-seven, she plans to continue working for at least five or six more years. "I will continue because I love the work I am doing that addresses the burdens carried by my race having had its humanity disavowed for so long as well as tracking the progress we have made as a people. With evidence generated and gathered from developmental science and other fields, we are challenging entrenched ways of thinking. I find that engaging in work that contributes to paradigmatic shifts, as a global model of change, is intellectually stimulating and highly energizing."

Since 2009 Margaret has held an endowed chair as Marshall Field IV Professor of Urban Education in the Comparative Human Development Department at the University of Chicago. Previous professorial positions were at Emory University (for sixteen years) and the University of Pennsylvania, Graduate School of Education and the School of Arts and Sciences (for sixteen years), where she also was honored with an endowed chair. "Of course, it is certainly gratifying to hold endowed chairs at prestigious institutions," she says, "but more important is having the opportunity to do my research and apply it in various settings, which can make a difference for young people."

Margaret teaches graduate and undergraduate courses on concepts and theories of human development; adolescent development; and race, ethnicity, and human development. She describes herself as "a basic social scientist, but unusual," in that she is equally committed to *applying knowledge programmatically.* "I love studying the puzzle of human development as it unfolds under diverse and stress-filled conditions, which vary relative to supports available, perceptions of same, and their character," she explains. Margaret is particularly interested in *resiliency predictors*—the complexity and play of risk factors and protective factors that influence whether outcomes for adolescents living in different and often adverse circumstances are healthy and constructive or the opposite.

Margaret first completed a five-year, chemistry-dominant degree program in pharmacy at Temple University in Philadelphia, becoming a registered pharmacist. She was one of very few women enrolled in the program at that time and found gender discrimination even more intractable than race issues. Following graduation and moving to the Midwest with her new husband, she decided to take a couple of courses in an unfamiliar field and was, ultimately, invited into a graduate degree program in psychology at the University of Kansas where she completed a master's degree. Her master's thesis recreated the famous Doll Test by Mamie and Kenneth Clark whose findings were cited in the 1954 *Brown v. Board of Education* decision. In the original 1939–1940 study, researchers Kenneth and Mamie Clark asked African American children to choose between black and white dolls to measure how segregation affected them. Replicating the study, Margaret learned more about racial identity formation given developmental processes during childhood: that color bias is learned as early as three years of age and that it can be modified with social incentives. Her advisor recommended her for a PhD program at the University of Chicago. She had a four-month-old baby and an eighteen-month-old toddler when she enrolled at the university but managed to complete her doctorate in child and developmental psychology in just five years.

Margaret's husband, an internal medicine doctor with a specialty in gerontology, earned both an MD and PhD (the latter in chemistry). At seventy-one, he continues to practice medicine as a clinical faculty member in the medical school at the University of Pennsylvania. The Drs. Spencer have three grown children. (Their two daughters have doctoral degrees; in fact, one daughter is also a University of Chicago MD PhD and is married to a UChicago PhD. Their son holds international patents and recently completed his MBA at Georgia Institute of Technology.) The Spencers have an energetic preschooler grandson on whom they dote. They like to get away to their vacation home on the Eastern Shore of Maryland, enjoy some international and stateside travel, as well as, at least dream about other places to travel around the globe. Margaret says she doesn't have time to think about the balance between her work, family, and leisure, she just does it all! And when the subject of retirement comes up, her husband just says, "Sure, sure. We'll talk about that after your sabbatical in 2012–2013."

In addition to the usual duties of a tenured professor—teaching and advising students, writing for many publications, directing grant-funded research projects, collaborating with partners on intervention efforts, and making pre-sentations at professional conferences and convocations—Margaret devotes time to community service because the work is very important to her. For example, she has been involved with a project in Philadelphia for eight years that seeks to improve the relationship between the criminal justice system and young people, notably boys of color, who are disproportionately apprehended by the police, and she also assists a residential care facility for young people in Detroit. Ever since she came of age in the 1960s, but even earlier during her years growing up in a Philadelphia housing project, Margaret has had a well-developed sense of purpose and a commitment to contribute to society. "Given the many challenges confronted in my own childhood and youth, I view my life as a special gift and, thus, *owe a great deal* for the opportunities enjoyed. That is what my life is all about . . . never forgetting, paying back, and *having no dissonance* about the knowledge-building advocacy role achieved through work."

Mentoring and coauthoring with postdocs, former students, and young people generally is another important but time-consuming responsibility. "I want to leave a legacy when I step down to ensure that the work goes on into the future. Positive change is based upon knowledge, culturally inclusive values, and the respect of all people. There is no doubt that race and social status continue to matter, especially as it impacts the achievement potential and health status of our young people. Thus, leaving a legacy of intellectual warriors is essential."

For a woman who claims "multitasking is my middle name," admitting that she cannot really do it all is not easy. Margaret finds that she cannot pull all-nighters anymore and she is becoming more cautious about taking on too much. "I am learning to say 'no' and refer speaking engagements, valued col-laborations, or professional opportunities to other people. It is important to pace yourself and do the things you really want to do and that you do best. Give over the things that can be done by others." In trying to get as much work done as possible (whether in Philadelphia, Chicago, or other locations), Margaret has had to make sacrifices over the years. She knows that she may have slighted some friends and not taken enough time to smell the roses. "I guess I am still in a 'training mode' about all this, but I am getting better!"

Another thing that Margaret has neglected is fitness; though she does try to watch what she eats, she has a sweet tooth. "Honestly, I think I am looking pretty good. My new bifocals blend in with my white hair, and I continue to receive compliments about my skin . . . I have no wrinkles. That is one of the benefits of being an older black woman . . . doing your passion and looking pretty good in the process!" she laughs. Margaret is clearly aging successfully both professionally and personally and none other than AARP agrees: its magazine's fall 2011 issue is highlighting seniors who are aging well and Margaret will be featured.

In many instances where a woman made a career change, the position she left was in teaching or administration in K–12 schools or at the college level, education being one of the careers these women were most often encouraged to choose from when they went to college. Fields left behind were also apt to be in the business world or in health care or social services. Former business positions were as follows: programmer analyst, scientific computer programmer, information services, software engineer, life insurance actuary, sales, financial services marketer, real estate broker, and travel agent. Former health care or social services jobs were: nurse, physical therapist, family therapist, and child life specialist. Other former positions included: minister, writer, lawyer, and chemist.

Jaye Moore is a career changer who found her true calling later in life. After a stint in nursing and time out for child rearing, Jaye began studying for the ministry in her fifties to fulfill her dream of becoming a hospice chaplain. Now she uses her special gifts in meeting the spiritual needs of dying patients and their family members, performing a job for which the demand is constant.

PROFILE: JAYE MOORE

On a recent warm spring day, Jaye Moore's husband started up his big heavy motorcycle and took Jaye for a ride in the countryside. "It's a blast! We need to do that once in a while for ourselves. Sometimes we harness up our horse, Penny, and go for a buggy ride," she grins. As an ordained minister and chaplain, Jaye usually covers the miles in an SUV. Like an old-fashioned circuit-riding judge, she travels throughout Boston's MetroWest towns to nursing homes, assisted-living facilities, private homes, hospice care centers—wherever hospice patients are—providing nondenominational spiritual support to patients, their families, and the staff who care for them. She conducts funerals and memorial services (occasional weddings and baptisms, too), and also fills in when chaplains in surrounding regions need her. She is on call any time. Arriving home from work at 10 p.m. is not unusual. "I really, really love what I do; it is very rewarding. If I am tired, it is a *good* tired!"

Medicare pays for a patient's hospice care and "drives the bus." Medicare requires an initial assessment, followed by interdisciplinary team reviews every two weeks to update patient care plans. Jaye does initial spiritual assessments and updates spiritual care plans to ensure that a patient's emotional pain and comfort are addressed along with physical needs.

Unlike most chaplains, Jaye is also a registered nurse. "I gave up a full scholarship to art school to get my RN because I wanted to help people. Art was a 'gift' that I could keep as a hobby." Nursing was her first career, but it turned out not to be her favorite. While she worked as an operating room supervisor, she pursued a bachelor's degree part time in English and psychology to better understand human behavior. She married an orthopedic surgeon and raised two children, but always in the back of her mind there was something else she felt she had to do, another calling: ministry.

Finally, in her fifties, and without the sponsorship of her Congregational church (the pastor blocked her request), Jaye enrolled in divinity school at the multifaith Andover-Newton Theological Seminary in Newton, Massachusetts, the oldest graduate seminary in America. Attending part time, she completed the three-year master's degree program in four years, then acquired an additional four years of experience in clinical pastoral education in Boston-area hospitals. "I wanted my ministry to be hands-on with small groups or one-on-one, not in a supervisory or administrative role, and not in a church pulpit," she explains.

Yet another year of training was devoted to feminist study in ministry at the Episcopal Divinity School in Cambridge, Massachusetts. Gender discrimination used to bother her, but now she is unruffled when a patient or family member tells her, "I do not want female clergy, I want a *man*," or when someone barks, "I want a *real* minister!"

In her first paid placement, Jaye often worked sixty hours in forty-hour weeks for low pay. "I was run ragged. What drove me away from that job was not working twenty extra hours for no pay, it was management's exclusive focus on the business side, on beating the competition and getting the numbers up, rather than on the quality of patient care." Her philosophy is doing the most good for the greatest number of people. "When I was ordained, I was told that you go when and where you are needed." What is most fulfilling about her chaplaincy is helping a hospice patient to die in peace, both spiritually and physically, even though it can be emotionally taxing for her. "I meet people where they are, no matter their faith or lack of faith. They trust me with their thoughts and fears." She also likes working with the families, helping them to accept the reality of the hospice situation, and assuring them that their loved one is comfortable. "A chaplain comes in at the end of life when family dynamics are often very challenging," she explains. "It can be especially hard when two patients in different facilities are dying at the same time and I am trying to be there for both of them."

Jaye thinks her age (sixty-eight) is just a number. Her advice to friends who hesitate about trying something new or getting a degree has always been, "You are going to be the same age whether you do it or not, so go for it!" She does like it when colleagues tell her that she does not look her age. "I do not want to be viewed as a little old lady!" She regularly undergoes continuing education and training in her field, as mandated by Medicare, and has mastered the complicated new software program used for documenting patient visits and status. "Medicare makes us very aware of the importance of documentation, dotting every 'i' and crossing every 't'." Jaye is modest about the recognition she has received for her dedication to caregiving. She was recently invited to speak about hospice at a Controversial Issues in Cancer Care seminar at the local hospital and chair a roundtable discussion on "Ethical Issues When Care Givers Disagree."

Ministry is a good job for an older woman, Jaye believes, and she expects to continue working until seventy-five or eighty, so long as she remains physically fit. (A hospice chaplain must undergo a mandatory physical exam every year.) If their grown children had their way, both Moore grandparents would be retired and able to travel more. Jaye and her husband used to go away on trips with a group of friends who enjoyed vigorous outdoor activities, but they always came back early to go to work. Now the Moores are the only ones in that social group who are still employed. At a minimum, her children think Jaye should save the weekends for family and leisure activities;

they do not like her to be on call when the family retreats to their vacation place in Maine. "We will talk about it . . . some day. I would not mind having time to write the great American novel—that would be fun. Maybe if the motor vehicle bureau does not allow us to renew the registration for the motorcycle or when Penny, our buggy horse, is ready to retire. At twenty-something, she is getting old, but she is still spirited and in good condition." Sound familiar?

Among the other late-starters in my study is a sixty-three-year-old university administrator and former faculty member who took time out for child rearing. "In my experience, women are stronger and can work longer than men. Their real careers begin at forty, and they can really contribute a lot in their later years. I know a good-sized number of women who have retired from the university and have been brought back to run various projects."

Opportunities for training, retraining, and updating skills appear to be minor reasons for continuing to work into one's senior years: only 11 percent cite this as a reason. Some women do not stop learning new skills or functions; they move from one career to another as their interests change and new opportunities arise. For example, a sixty-two-year-old self-employed part-time watercolor instructor makes this point: "I can't imagine ever *not* working at all. I felt like I 'retired' at age thirty-four when I quit my full-time job as a management consultant/trainer and became a freelance magazine writer—so much more freedom! I had been a family therapist before that, and worked in a hospital before that. Then I got into travel photography, which became yet another career. Later I took up watercolor on a lark, and it has become a whole new four-day-a-week career for me, teaching adults who are absolute beginners and improving my own painting skills."

My invitation to share other reasons for remaining in the paid workforce elicited a veritable flood of heartfelt responses. The sampling that follows positively shouts with gusto and passion:

"The joy of it all!"

"Positive and meaningful connection to my community (town) for fifty-two years."

"My clients need me!"

"I love my work."

"It is fun!"

"I love what I do, am well paid, and have intrinsic rewards."

"Am healthy and really like what I do."

"There is work I want to do—so many ideas!"

"Validation, self-worth."

"Like to set and achieve goals."

"Sense of accomplishment and well-being."

"Status in paid employment/work. Work has always been part of my personal identity."

"Too much energy—still."

"Paying for third child's college education."

"Love, love the stimulation!"

The verve of these comments reminds me of Jules Feiffer's approach to life, as described in a review of the cartoonist's new memoir, *Backing into Forward*: "While other accomplished men bronze their success or dip it in amber, Feiffer treats his own as one big, wonderful caper." To apply the word "caper" to older working women is not to imply any lack of seriousness or intensity on their part (or men's, for that matter). Quite the contrary. In other words, one can delight in one's achievements without becoming smug.[6]

Along with the joy and passion, of course, there are often family responsibilities, competing demands on one's time, financial and health concerns, and issues in the workplace to contend with, as we shall see in chapter 8.

Personal Challenges and Concerns

To know how to grow old is the master work of wisdom, and one of the most difficult chapters in the great art of living.—Henri Frederic Amiel, Swiss philosopher, poet, critic (1821–1881)

Working into one's sixties and seventies is not all fun and games, of course. Many older working women confess to experiencing a little or a lot of stress and fatigue (44 percent). One woman admits that a recent move has been a challenge. And yet another points out that she takes care of a great deal in addition to her household responsibilities because she runs a big art show to raise money for children with autism. Working fifty hours a week is not unheard of. The president and executive director of a nonprofit organization loves her work, yet describes it as a "demanding job that can't be done effectively within a normal work week." An investment adviser wrestles with the regulatory burden in her field and the stress related to managing other people's money.

Respondents penned a variety of other comments regarding personal concerns. One out of three is worrying about the declining value of her investments or has suffered other financial setbacks. Their age or income level may put them beyond the reach of "exploding" mortgages and homes that are "underwater," yet they know that their children are vulnerable. In some cases the needs of grown children are just plain burdensome. One woman admits feeling this way: "Adult children's need for financial help—will it ever stop?" Others are terribly worried about grown children who have lost their jobs during the recession. They are happy to help their children with expenses, such as contributing to a grandchild's college tuition. However, when grandma pays the bills (or allows offspring and their children to move back home), instead of grown children looking out for *her*, it upends the whole idea of a "sandwich" generation.

Since my respondents have themselves moved into the senior ranks, only a small fraction of them have elderly or infirm family members to care for. Maxine Greenwald is a perfect example. At seventy-one she holds two jobs and is responsible for her mother and an extended family.

PROFILE: MAXINE GREENWALD

When your mother is ninety-seven, still playing word games on the computer, lives with you, and depends on you as her sole support, you cannot retire. When you have three children and fourteen grandchildren who count on your help, especially during the recession, you cannot retire. When you love your work and are really good at what you do, you don't want to retire. When you need the benefits that are accruing year by year, you will put off retirement. And when you are afraid to retire because you would have to build a whole new life, you just do not go there.

All this describes Maxine Greenwald, a veteran fifth grade teacher in Passaic, New Jersey, who also has a second job as a literacy teacher in an after-school program. The low-performing district is under close scrutiny by the state, and the pressure on teachers and students to produce is intense. "I know I help children every day," she affirms. "I am seventy-one but they don't think of me as old. Perhaps some of the Hispanic and Filipino teachers show me extra deference—it's a cultural thing."

Maxine says matter-of-factly, "I'm always on the cutting edge—I wouldn't stay in the field unless I was. If you're older and in the workforce, you have to keep up with the kids." When a new principal arrived four years ago and insisted that everything be done electronically—lesson plans, e-mail, and so on—that was stressful, Maxine admits. She acquired her own computer and doggedly mastered the essentials with her husband's help. "My principal did me a tremendous favor by catapulting me into the twenty-first century cyberworld!"

Maxine has been in the workforce for thirty-eight years. Years ago, she and her husband Harry ran a travel agency. When "the bottom dropped out" they had to sell it. Maxine, who really disliked the business world, gladly returned to her first love, teaching. When she originally began to work in Passaic, the population was middle class and blue collar, with mostly Jewish families. Gradually, the demographics changed and the city became heavily minority and poor. Their neighborhood has completely changed as well. What had been a huge circle of friends diminished as people died or relocated. The neighbors are now much, much younger. "That has been the hardest adjustment for me. The two of us are still here, the last of the Mohicans. I don't know people our age who are as flexible as we are," she says ruefully.

Her husband held several jobs after the travel agency closed, then he caught the teaching bug, enrolled in an alternative certification program, and became a technology coordinator in a different school in Passaic.

"We're having a wonderful time," Maxine explains. "We're role models for our kids and grandkids. They respect what we're doing, and I think they like us as people, and that's no small thing." She and her husband are the loving center of a traditional and observant Jewish family, hosting twenty-five adults and children for the Passover seder and other gatherings.

Maxine believes she was a sort of reverse role model for her mother, who never had a college education or enjoyed the advantages her daughter had. "I was everything my mother couldn't be. She worked because she had to—helping my father in his small retail store—and was ashamed of it. In her era a woman was supposed to stay home and keep house. Her parents were immigrants and their goal was assimilation to the American way."

Harry and Maxine, teaching's dynamic duo, plan to keep working as long as they have the health and stamina for it. "We're so busy," Maxine tells Harry, "we have no time to get old!" They share the household chores, since Maxine has conceded that she can't do everything by herself. She still measures her self-worth largely by what she can accomplish in a day. She thrives on keeping a busy schedule and being useful. "It's fun to put all the pieces together. There's no stress when it's so enjoyable, not like stress in the business world." Fortunately, the recession has not affected them directly; they live modestly. She believes that it's important to listen to an "inner voice" that tells you what to do, what feels right. "If you enjoy the path you're on, go for it. It will keep you young."

Although a knee problem curtails how far she walks (she used to jog four miles a day), Maxine lives by a metaphor she heard in a song that speaks of choosing between sitting it out or dancing. She and Harry are choosing to dance.

Adult caregiving is part of the history of a sixty-one-year-old woman who is now a part-time librarian. She recalls the twenty-four-year period when she was looking after her mother: "Caregiving responsibilities were very intense while my mother lived in my home and I had to care for her twenty-four/ seven and work full time as a high school teacher and manage rental properties and take care of a large home and grounds." Few of the women I surveyed are caregivers for grandchildren. Those who do help out with their grandchildren typically say the time commitment is light.

Presently, the loss of friends or loved ones seems to be a relatively infrequent occurrence among the women I studied, but one that hovers ominously in the background and is sure to weigh more heavily as the years go by. Poignantly, for one seventy-nine-year-old woman, the increased frailty of her friends and loved ones has become a major concern.

A frequent regret is not having enough time for family, friends, and outside activities. Many especially regret the lack of time with children and grandchildren, who often live at a distance. When schedules are tight, creative, cultural, and social interests outside of work, such as music, theater, painting, reading, writing, exercising, enjoying the outdoors, entertaining and seeing friends, too often must be sacrificed. "Not enough travel time, hobby time, and hanging-out-doing-nothing-time," laments one woman. A seventy-four-year-old observes, "It takes time to manage Medicare and to maintain good health and my walking routine." Yet another woman reasons, "Most of my friends who are retired and taking classes for fun invite me to join them. I am trying to maintain those relationships, so I take time from work. I'm juggling work and play but can't really participate much in all the fun activities they plan. So I fear that my friends find other friends to hang out with. Basically, not much time is 'spare' when you have your own private practice to run. I would take more classes and do more volunteering or participate in a charity, but I work twenty-four/seven, so it's not possible."

Karen Shaeffer, whose profile you are about to read, knew she did not want to look back on her later years filled with regret that she had not seen parts of the globe that fascinated her. Unlike the older working women mentioned previously, she figured out a way to be both gainfully employed *and* a world traveler.

PROFILE: KAREN SHAEFFER

Calling one's blog "Ma Prochaine Aventure" (i.e., "My Next Adventure") tells a lot about a person, and this is true of Karen Sheaffer, who has just signed up to teach for a third year in Dakar, Senegal. Karen is a kindergarten teacher at the International School of Dakar. She enjoys the direct work with children and the new experiences of living and traveling in Africa.

When her last full-time job in the Boston area ended in June 2009, Karen did not feel ready to retire. She had not taught in the classroom for many years and often thought she would like to do that again. She also wanted to travel. She is very happy to be working at the International School of Dakar. Relearning French is a plus—she had studied in France as an undergraduate, but that was more than forty-five years ago, so her foreign language skills had become more than a little rusty. The school pays for French lessons once a week. She also receives free housing—a three-bedroom, three and a half bath furnished apartment for her and her little dog—and the paid utilities. There is full-time maid service and her maid practices French with her and teaches her words in Wolof, the local language. Her French is improving, but she finds that local people are much friendlier when she greets them in Wolof with "*na nga def.*"

Except for the hot, rainy season, she finds the weather in Dakar to be ideal. Among other perks is the large outdoor pool located right next to the school. "I have always been a swimmer and used to pay about $1,000 to belong to a club with a good pool. Here the club costs only $200 for the year!"

During her free time she has traveled to Togo and Burkina Faso in West Africa where she visited rural schools, shopped in colorful fabric markets, and ate a dish of pounded yams known as *fufu*. She toured coffee and cocoa plantations and a hydroelectric dam. She went to a leper colony whose residents use the batik method to print fabric and to a workshop and training center for women where they learn to make soap, weave, and sew clothing. She takes excursions accompanied by a guide/translator and some of the other "ex-pat" teachers and nurses who live in her apartment building. Last year, they visited Lac Rose, a vast shallow lagoon northeast of Dakar and known for its pink-hued waters and its unusually high salt content.

Karen told me about her background. With a master's degree in education from Tufts University and a Certificate of Advanced Graduate Study from Wheelock College, Karen was well qualified for the many positions she held in the ECE field over the years. When she turned sixty, Karen had no thought of teaching abroad. She was working as a freelance consultant and trainer for the Boston Institute for Arts Therapy "Raising Readers" training project and for the Family Child Care Training Project at the Children's Museum. She conducted Head Start program reviews and also led professional development workshops for teachers and paraprofessionals and taught classes at the college level in day care administration, special education, child growth and development, infant toddler curriculum, and more. "At that point, I felt and looked terrific. To celebrate my sixtieth birthday, I trained and did the New York to Boston AIDS bike ride—four days of hard cycling! Then I did the AIDS bike ride every summer after that until I moved to Senegal."

Ironically, it was the recession that gave Karen the impetus and the wherewithal to make some major changes in her life. "The recession was the reason why my job ended in the United States and I began looking for a teaching job overseas. So the effect was very positive for me. Also, my (then) husband and I sold our house right before the real estate decline, which gave us the money to afford to divorce in 2008 and start our new lives. While the recession benefitted me in those ways, I do worry about my children whose finances were negatively affected by the downturn."

Changes both professional and personal opened up new opportunities for Karen. "The move into consulting and freelance work was successful. Physically I felt energized and in peak condition. I expanded my circle of friends and activities. And after the divorce I made my own decisions about where to live, how to decorate my apartment, which car to buy, etc."

Although relocating overseas was a very good decision for Karen, moving from teaching adults to teaching children again was a struggle. "I am learning so much in the process and reevaluating many of the teaching practices I once used." She is pleased to see the positive influence she is having on the young children she teaches at the International School, just as she was proud of the results she got from working with and teaching adult providers in ECE.

Living far from her two children and the rest of her family is the hardest part of Karen's new life in Africa. "I miss them so much. Because of the time change, and their work schedules, I don't get to talk to them as often as I would like. Fortunately, my sister and her husband have just arrived in Dakar to spend two months here—instead of their usual winter trip to Florida." Karen's family and friends back home in Cambridge and Brookline, Massachusetts, completely support her decision to move to Dakar and to keep working there. "They often say they are jealous of my adventures!"

Perhaps to compensate for the absence of her loved ones, Karen makes connections with other people through her leisure activities. "Most people have no idea how old I am, and if I tell them, they are shocked! I do not look or feel old among younger colleagues because I have the same interests and do many of the same things that they do." Every other week, she plays cards with some of the other teachers. Once a week she goes to French class after school. Once a month a group of teachers gets together to dine, going to all sorts of different restaurants in Dakar.

And, Karen loves her book group, which she finds "so much more diverse than my book group was in the states. It is one of the aspects of working at the International School that I especially like. We have several reading groups that meet monthly to discuss a book. I am in the group that is reading *The Biological Brain in a Cultural Classroom*. Last summer I attended a one-week institute on the writing process offered by the US State Department Office of Overseas Schools."

While maintaining good health and fitness is as important to Karen as it is to most of us as we age, one thing that is not going as well as she would like is her workout regimen. "I have reduced the amount and frequency of my swimming. I used to swim three-quarters of a mile every day. Now I only do half-mile swims a couple of times a week. Two and a half years ago I developed severe arthritis in my knees, so I am also doing much less walking than I used to do. Bike riding is easier for me. I am thinking about knee replacement surgery after I return to the United States in June 2012. I just hope the knees hold out until then!"

Karen's contract ends and she will turn seventy in 2012. She has decided to retire then to have more time to travel and do some of the things that she cannot do now because of her work schedule. With her usual verve, Karen concluded the interview with the following advice for other women who are considering working and adventuring beyond age sixty: "Only do what you enjoy, keep learning, and try new things."

Karen Shaeffer seems to be enjoying everything about the work she chose, except being so far away from kith and kin, and that is only temporary. However, when asked about personal challenges and concerns pertaining to their jobs, quite a few of her peers in my study are forthright about issues regarding changes in and demands of the workplace. A sixty-eight-year-old realtor admits to struggling to keep up with new technologies. "I've also had to adjust to my younger clients' need for instant communication." An RN in obstetrics and gynecology concurs: "At my age (sixty-eight), staff nursing is very rewarding, but it's also more difficult to keep up with new technology and responsibilities!" A sixty-three-year-old part-time speech/language pathologist admits: "Highest pay, yes. Seniority and respect in my field, yes. But less at peak in technology and new tools despite continuing education." Another sixty-eight-year-old feels disrespected. "There's an occasional negative climate at work. My status as a clerical or 'permanent temp' employee has diminished my stature in colleagues' eyes." She is one of nineteen women in my study who say they are bothered by a pervasively negative organizational climate. A college professor in her early sixties finds department chairing incredibly time consuming. "It feels like more than a full-time job and a somewhat thankless one at that. I'm looking forward to stepping down in June and going on sabbatical next year. Then I'll return to full-time teaching, directing, and advising. I'm not ready to retire yet, but I'm eager to spend more time with my grandchildren."

Sometimes outright misfortune strikes and a career woman is sorely tested. A sixty-year-old full-time self-employed attorney discloses her predicament: "I am currently at a crossroads in my professional life. My law partner is dying of brain cancer and no longer works. When our lease expired in fall 2009, I closed the office and moved all the files to my home. Soon I will need to make a decision as to what I want to do with the rest of my professional life as I do not see being a solo practitioner as a viable option for many reasons."

Just 21 percent say that they have no personal challenges or concerns at this time. "My challenge is perhaps not really a negative—there are so many wonderful options, things to do!" exclaims a sixty-eight-year-old psychotherapist. "There is work I want to do—so many ideas!" echoes a sixty-eight-year-old studio artist.

And If There Is Time to Spare . . .

Volunteers are the only human beings on the face of the earth who reflect this nation's compassion, unselfish caring, patience, and just plain love for one another.—Erma Bombeck

A little over one-fourth of all Americans, nearly 63 million people, performed some type of volunteer work at least once in 2010, says the US BLS. This was a rate that was largely unchanged from 2007 and 2008. The greatest number (35.1 percent) were volunteering in religious institutions; followed by education/youth service (26 percent); social or community service (13.5 percent); hospital or other health service (8.2 percent); civic, political, professional, or international service (5.5 percent). Lesser numbers were volunteering in "other" ways, involving sports, hobbies, cultural or arts organizations, environmental initiatives, animal care, and public safety.[1]

On the one hand, it is understandable that older professional women might not have time for volunteer service. "*What* spare time? I maintain my home and health and oversee my family's legal and financial matters," one woman scrawled on her survey. On the other hand, more than half of her peers (52 percent) are doing a remarkable amount of volunteering. That this is more than double the national average reported by the BLS can perhaps be explained by older women's strong sense of civic, social, and religious engagement, or perhaps it is merely their freedom from child care responsibilities.

For an example of civic engagement, let's recall what chapter 7 revealed about Dr. Margaret Beale Spencer's well-developed sense of purpose and commitment to contribute to society: "Given the many challenges confronted in my own childhood and youth, I view my life as a special gift and, thus, *owe a great deal* for the opportunities enjoyed. That is what my life is all about—never forgetting, paying back."

Community service and serving on boards or cultural councils are most popular among the women in my study, followed by: church- or synagogue-related activities, such as serving as clerk of a Quaker meeting; political activity; fundraising for one's *alma mater* or other organization; tutoring and teaching; working in a food pantry, museum, history center, YMCA, or library; and driving patients to doctors' appointments. Older working women are volunteering as hospice helpers and grief support providers and assisting organizations for people with disabilities. I also learned about a mentor for people with food allergies, a reader for a blind person, a coordinator of a free vision and medical program for indigent families, a presenter to students on the Holocaust, a bookkeeper for Planned Parenthood, a leader of teams building homes in developing countries, a Best Buddy for a middle school student, and a friend for a person who has mental health issues.

Betty Funk may be the paradigmatic older working woman who successfully divides her time among her consulting business, hearth and home, professional and social networks, and community service. Somehow she gets it all done, and beautifully.

PROFILE: BETTY FUNK

Elizabeth (Betty) Funk is a great-grandmother three times over and is in semiretirement, but you would never know it. After eight years as executive director of the Youth Guidance Center (Greater Framingham Mental Health Association), she served as president and CEO of Mental Health and Substance Abuse Corporations of Massachusetts (MHSACM, since renamed the Association of Behavioral Health Care). Her cause was educating society about mental health and supporting policy and funding to create access to high-quality treatment for children, adults, and families. She was such a presence at the State House in Boston that the legislators took to calling the advocacy organization the "Betty Funk Club." She also chaired the board of the National Council for Community Behavioral Health Care in Washington, D.C., and remains an active member.

When her husband had a health crisis three years ago, she spent more time at home but dreaded the idea of retirement. She shifted from a nearly twenty-four/seven work schedule to a part-time consulting business called ELF Consulting (the title represents her initials, not her stature) at which she works about one-quarter time for pay and the rest pro bono. Part connector, part maven, part saleswoman, she exemplifies traits journalist and author Malcolm Gladwell describes in *The Tipping Point²* by deftly linking people and resources and helping to make things happen. It helps to know everybody and everything on the national behavioral health scene. Board governance, her specialty, is the focus of her current consulting work and her conference presentations.

Betty's goals when she was young were crystal clear: (1) marry someone she was passionately in love with, (2) have a bunch of kids, (3) live in a big white house with a halo over it, (4) finish college, and (5) participate in community service. She has done it all. First, the husband (when she was not yet twenty) and three kids in quick succession. Next, with or without the halo, the house—truly a photographer's dream. A Colonial dating to 1665, it has wide plank flooring and an attached barn that the Funks shopped for all over New England. They had it moved in pieces and reassembled on site, rough-hewn beams and all, and did much of the renovation work themselves.

Returning to school was next. In her thirties Betty was working full time at MHSACM, which she was building into a powerhouse, while taking college courses at night. "The lack of credentials haunted me and forced me to reassess my sense of self. It was a real turning point." Even before she had completed her undergraduate studies, Simmons College accepted her into the innovative Program in Management for Women where she excelled. "That was *so* challenging. Working in Boston, studying . . . I never had enough sleep!" Earning the MBA at forty-five prompted another reassessment, another turning point. "My feet never touched ground for three years. The Simmons deans wanted their students to break the 'glass ceiling' by heading up banks, insurance firms, computer companies, or the like. At that time, health and human services were not on their radar screen. However, I had decided that I wasn't after money or fame. I was going to build an amazing career in behavioral health."

The fifth goal was accomplished along the way. She became heavily involved in community service: the League of Women Voters, Town Meeting (a traditional form of government in New England towns), and the hospital board. A hospital merger and then a sale, negotiations, the trials and tribulations of shaping managed care, budgetary and capital issues—all prepared her to "be at the table" on the state and national level in health care reform because she understood the language of the business and had a gift for explaining the physical health-behavioral health interface. Along the way, she amassed an "embarrassingly" long list of state and national leadership awards.

Her proudest achievements? There are several. "The high moment was walking across the stage to accept my MBA degree. The League of Women Voters work taught me so much. Forming and building the MHSACM providers' association was a major accomplishment, as was helping to shape the health care system and ensuring the survival of our community hospital."

Her goals at age seventy are simpler but equally challenging. She wants to achieve some equilibrium and go at a gentler pace. "I am teaching myself to say 'no' and to stop caring about so many different things. I'd like to surround myself with people and issues that I enjoy and at the same time find quiet space to read historical novels, solve a crossword puzzle, garden, play golf, travel, or do absolutely nothing with satisfaction." However, the gentler pace may have to wait a while, for Betty chairs her town's "FinComm" (finance committee), an extremely demanding volunteer job, especially in these economically depressing times. She attends board meetings of the national behavioral health care council in Washington, D.C., and shares her expertise in behavioral health policy, financing, and clinical systems. At home, she's active with the local art museum and the history center. A beloved husband of fifty-two years, three children, and their families (five grandchildren and three great-grandbabies) are the center of her personal life. She is the person a grandson asks to sew up the holes in his lacrosse gloves.

She knows her husband would like her to be around more. He retired ten years ago after a lengthy engineering career that frequently took him to Japan and elsewhere and left his wife managing everything on her own. In her experience, "women with families tend to start their careers later than men, so when husbands are eager to retire, wives are just reaching their peak and still raring to go." Since her husband's retirement, two open heart surgeries have forced him to be more cautious. "He loves being at home and managing the house," Betty explains. "He does his things, I do mine. He has his office, I have mine. We need to do more *together.*"

Betty's ninety-nine-year-old mother definitely thinks her daughter should do less. "Do different things and do things differently," is her advice. Mother, who lives independently in her own house in Maryland, once worked for Ernie Pyle, the famous war correspondent. She married and raised five children in the World War II era. When her husband died in his mid-fifties, she joined the many women from her neighborhood working at the Washington Suburban Sanitary Commission. Together they kept an eye on one another's children. She planted a garden (as did many who lived through the Depression) and was frugal. Later she was able to travel all over the world.

Her mother's motto—"keep moving, keep involved"—and her positive mental attitude have clearly rubbed off on Betty. "A positive attitude and good health are what you have going for you." Because of her husband's heart problems, Betty stopped working full time. Nevertheless, she believes women should work as long as they can. They tend to live longer than men and will need to support themselves into old age. Be independent but stay connected both professionally and socially with interesting people who challenge you intellectually. That way, you think *outwardly* and focus less on personal matters. And then this remarkable high achiever shares one lingering regret: "I feel that I never did enough. I should have taken a position in Washington, but it just didn't fit in my family plan."

Betty Funk is not the only volunteer *par excellence* among the older working women I studied. One intrepid sixty-six-year-old who works part time as an educational consultant also helps run a café at arts center concerts, ushers for the local Philharmonic Orchestra, is a volunteer staffer for her NPR-related radio station, serves on a board, is a liaison to UNICEF, and performs pro bono consulting for a small nonprofit child care center.

Another sixty-six-year-old who is a full-time professor says that she often performs volunteer work that falls outside the norm: "In my kind of work, the line between what counts as leisure and what counts as work really blurs. I do a great deal that is not in my job description, but that does not count under conventional definitions of volunteering or public service—even though it has substantial public dimensions."

Leisure time activities are no less important to these older professional women. They may be putting their feet up while they relax, but they are nearly all reading books (and increasingly, e-books) at the same time (85 percent). No wonder the book club phenomenon—all-female or coed groups—is alive and well. Most of the members of my book group, myself included, also belong to a second book group that meets in a library, a bookstore, or a private home.

They also like to be on the go—more than two-thirds travel (68 percent). More than half engage in sports and fitness activities (54 percent), including camping and hiking. Some prefer surf fishing, snowshoeing, horseback riding, or yoga. One woman simply takes long walks to clear her mind.

Mental exercise is just as important. This already highly educated set seeks out learning opportunities. Three women are pursuing advanced degrees (for credit) on top of their work schedules. Nearly one-third are enrolled in adult education (noncredit) courses. For example, a sixty-seven-year-old psychotherapist takes *and* teaches peer learning courses in her spare time at the Institute for Retired Professionals at The New School in New York City.

Another New Yorker is one of the PhD candidates who responded to my survey. When I interviewed Laurel Ann Wilson, known as Lauri, she was completing her dissertation on the Birth of Fashion in the Fourteenth Century and preparing to defend it before her doctoral committee. She had just turned sixty-five.

PROFILE: LAUREL ANN WILSON

Lauri has been a PhD candidate at Fordham University since the mid-1990s. Before she could start doctoral studies she had to complete the final year of college, which she had walked away from years earlier. She was nearly fifty when she returned to school (at Hunter College this time) to finish her credits. She knew she was too old to start an academic career, even with a doctorate, so she undertook graduate study simply for her own satisfaction. "I have a passion for medieval history. You have to have a passion, or it is too hard. It is like the love I have for the theater. My parents took me to see a play called *The*

Disenchanted when I was twelve years old, and I was transported forever by the experience. Years later I had another eureka moment when I was in Paris, wandering around Notre Dame Cathedral reading a book about the Middle Ages. I decided then and there to become a historian of the Middle Ages, and I have never looked back. I am into material culture—what objects can tell us about the societies they come from. It is an area that involves the study of anthropology, economics, art, and more. It is interdisciplinary and fascinating!"

Although she has never lost sight of her scholarly goal, Lauri has had some major setbacks along the way. A few years ago she was diagnosed with attention deficit disorder (ADD). "In the process of looking for a dissertation coach, I found a person who also happened to provide coaching to people with ADD. That is how I finally discovered that I was not bad or stupid or crazy." Then Lauri's ninety-four-year-old mother, for whom she was caring, had a stroke and was moved into a nursing home. And all this time Lauri has been holding down her full-time job as house manager at the Booth Theater, which is one of the oldest and smallest of the Shubert Theaters on the Great White Way.

Here is the back story. Lauri has lived in Manhattan for most of her sixty-five years. Her father was the archetypical ad man straight out of the 1950s "Mad Men" era. When she was little, her dad would take her along with him when he visited the sets of live television shows. Lauri loved the charged atmosphere. A little later, at sleepaway camp, a drama counselor noticed Lauri brooding over something and, to get her mind off the problem, invited her to the theater. Lauri quickly discovered that many of the campers who hung out at the theater were "misfits," but it did not really bother her. She was right at home there.

After graduating from a boarding school she describes as "Auntie Mame-ish"—very free-form and unconventional—where she excelled academically and was class valedictorian, Lauri decided, at the age of fifteen, to start college in another state. Her parents told her that she was too young, but she would not listen to their advice. She did not complete the freshman year. "I quickly realized it was a big mistake. I came home and took an acting class. I thought I could be a director, but that was not to be. I took a speedwriting class and got a secretarial job at Doubleday and Company, earning $75 a week. I was all of sixteen." Next, Lauri attended Barnard College as an art history major. She was involved in theater management in college as president of the Gilbert and Sullivan Society, but dropped out of school after three years because she refused to complete Barnard's physical education requirements.

Fortunately, with her secretarial training, it was easy to land a job taking dictation for a theatrical producer. He noticed that she was able to spell correctly and invited her to be his assistant. In this way she met people who noticed her aptitude for various management duties and that eventually led to twenty years as a general manager of Broadway shows. She was one of the first women, and the youngest, to general manage a Broadway show. After deciding to go back to school, she moved into house managing eighteen years ago. "Being a general manager is a tough twenty-four-hour per day job. You have to worry about everything and take it all home with you. In comparison, the house manager has an easier time of it." For the past ten years she has been the house manager at the Booth Theater, supervising all the "front of the house" staff, such as the box office, bookkeeping, payroll, porters and cleaners, and seeing to customer safety and service. "If you break your leg, I will be the one to call an ambulance," she informed me with a laugh.

This house manager is not above mopping up puddles. Once when a burst pipe flooded part of the theater, Lauri immediately pitched in to clean up the mess. Suddenly, a friend of her mother's appeared directly in front of Lauri and announced in an imperious voice, "I am going to tell your mother what you *really* do!"

Lauri does not regret remaining single and not having children. Her one big regret is that she has ignored her personal life for too many years. She has to be at the theater for every single performance, and her days are spent working on her dissertation. She used to enjoy hosting dinner parties and entertaining friends, but she has lost touch with most of them. She has had no time for movies, no time to fix up her apartment, or do much of anything else besides the theater. Her only day off during the long run of the hit drama *Next to Normal* was on Wednesday, though not much social life was to be had on Wednesdays.

Once Lauri has finished her doctorate, she plans to take a trip to Paris with a college roommate who is a composer of microtonal music and opera. The friend keeps telling Lauri to stop working at the theater and concentrate on medieval history. In the friend's opinion, scholarship is a more creative endeavor and nothing should interfere with that. However, Lauri tells her friend that she will keep working at the theater as long as she can. "I need to have a schedule. I need the outside contact, the opportunity to socialize with theater people and patrons. What's more, the job pays well, has great benefits, and is not physically demanding."

Lauri is also planning an academic conference with her dissertation advisor and hopes to teach a class at Fordham on medieval history as expressed through fashion. She will try to turn her dissertation into a publishable book.

As a theater manager, Lauri is proudest of the levels she achieved in her career. "Before I worked at the Booth, I had opened an office in the Shubert Building. However, it was hard to be finding new clients and doing the work at the same time. I moved pretty high up in the theater management world at a time when women were not expected to be in charge there. Ultimately, I was not successful when I went out on my own. I was not sufficiently detail oriented—maybe because of the ADD or maybe not—and I had difficulty delegating. That cost me a terrific job I had for nine years with Joe Papp and his fabulous Shakespeare Festival. Luckily, serendipity intervened and I met an old acquaintance in the Sardi Building elevator who helped me get my next position. I was very lucky: there are only thirty-five Broadway theaters and there are not very many openings."

Lauri comes from a long line of women who look younger than their real age. "Turning sixty-five really threw me. People say I do not look sixty-five. I am in the cohort of the oldest baby boomers, but most of the time I feel like an adolescent and think about all the many things I still want to do! I worried about being so much older than the other students at grad school when I was getting started, then I decided to ignore my age and simply fit in, and I did."

Lauri's busy schedule has caused her to neglect taking care of herself; she admits to being overweight and having minor physical ailments. On the other hand, she is in pretty good shape financially: she could stop working if she wanted to or had to. The economic downturn is hurting the theater business. *Next to Normal* did very well and kept her employed at the Booth all through the recession years until the play finally closed in mid-winter 2011. Another show is coming to her theater, but it is hard to know how long it will stay. "Theater management is a dicey business. We are forever being hired and laid off as shows come and go."

But the real reasons Lauri intends to keep working are twofold. First, as mentioned previously, she has learned how important it is to interact with other people at the theater instead of isolating herself as a scholar. And second, she appreciates what the theater does for her. It is never the same. There is never a dull moment. "When I went to work at Doubleday at age sixteen, I met a woman named Lucy in the research department who worked on a comptometer. That was a powerful type of adding machine with an oversized carriage that allowed you to see the numbers across a page. (Today we would call Lucy a data entry operator.) She had been there doing that for forty years. I knew right away that whatever I was going to do, it would not be the same thing for forty boring years. And I was right about that!"

Just under one-third of the women I studied say they enjoy solving crosswords and other puzzles in their spare time. More than one-third (38 percent) use computers, the Internet, e-mail, blogs, or social media. Writing is another favored pastime, and for some, writing makes a contribution to the knowledge base in their field. One early childhood educator writes articles and book chapters. Another early childhood specialist generates film critiques, responds to professional listserv queries, and collects news clips on education, parenting, family policy, children and the media, and more. A university faculty development director publishes books and articles.

It is apparent that these older women appear to have gotten the message that exercise—both mental and cardiovascular—promotes brain health. A healthy brain is their meal ticket. Exercise aids learning and memory, protects from neurodegeneration, and alleviates depression, *especially in older adults.* The Society for Neuroscience tells us that the brain can create new brain cells (neurons) in adulthood. Researchers have observed the process (neurogenesis) in the brain region involved in learning and memory. The brain's ability to create and modify networks of neurons is called plasticity. Neuroscientists report that a rich, stimulating environment—one filled with regular social interaction, exercise, and a healthful diet—can enhance versatility and adaptability and maintain brain plasticity, *even in old age.*[3]

A *New York Times'* March 2010 special section on retirement featured "the graying of the gym." Remarkably, the fastest growing segment of the health club population is adults fifty-five and older, now 10.5 million compared to 1.5 million in 1987.[4] Gym membership is not only for baby boomers who grew up in an exercise culture, but also for men and women in their seventies and eighties who are paying close attention to their physical fitness. The *Times* Personal Health columnist cites recent studies showing that regular exercise can prevent late-life disabilities. Physical activity reduces the odds of getting cancer, osteoporosis and fragility, cardiovascular disease, diabetes, and dementia.[5] As a regular walker, I was delighted to learn recently that walking for forty minutes three times a week can increase the size of the hippocampal area of the brain and improve one's memory. I was not so happy to hear that the crossword puzzles I like to work on every day have little or no protective effect.

After reading, traveling, sports and fitness, and computer usage come the more "traditional" uses of free time for older women in my study. In addition to home care and home decorating, gardening is a favorite pastime. A kitchen and bath designer is active in two garden clubs where she "happens" to meet potential clients. Other traditional hobbies such as knitting, needlepoint, and quilting have by no means been forgotten. Nonwork hours may also be devoted to religious worship or church- or synagogue-related programming, such as directing the adult choir or leading a women's group. Many make time for cultural events, such as lectures, films, or concerts, theater and dance performances, plus museum programs. And, of course, socializing in many forms makes the list—visiting friends, connecting with or simply keeping in touch with friends, playing bridge and other card games, entertaining (shopping, cooking, and baking), and spending time with family, especially children and grandchildren.

A few individuals mention less common ways to spend available time. A self-employed realtor in her late sixties manages a Christmas tree farm business with her husband ("it is both fun *and* work"). A woman in her mid-sixties, who has a banking background and is currently a product manager for long-term care insurance, has an investment club. A sixty-year-old university provost whose children are out on their own is training and caring for her new puppy, which she refers to as "my empty nest therapy purchase!"

10

Women Still at Work

I am trying to work out my fears and hopes about the Old Woman—who she is, what she's like, what she's capable of. These days when I walk into a public place with Ann . . . eyes gravitate to her and I get a taste of being invisible. I've waved away such moments, uncomfortable that I've even noticed them, but today I paused to see exactly what it was I felt. It wasn't envy, I realized. Rather, it felt like I'd just handed off my youth baton and now I get to go sit on the bench.—Sue Monk Kidd and Ann Kidd Taylor, *Traveling with Pomegranates: A Mother-Daughter Story*

"On the bench" or "on the shelf." Either expression connotes an unwelcome sidelining. In their dual memoir, author Sue Monk Kidd and her daughter, Ann Kidd Taylor, each try to find missing pieces of themselves as well as renewing the mother-daughter bond they both want and need, all while traveling together in Greece and France and retracing the mythical paths of Demeter and Persephone. Ann has just graduated from college and is in a quandary over what comes next. Sue is fifty, menopausal, and fearful about aging, loss of the creative spark, and her daughter's depression.[1]

At what age does a woman start to get a taste of being invisible? Sue Monk Kidd was already worrying about it when she was "only" fifty and a successful writer. What does a person without a job reply when asked the question so often posed upon first being introduced—And What Do You Do? She might say, "I used to . . . ," or "I am looking for . . . ," or "I am semi-retired." Finding a place in the paid workforce today, no matter how big or how small, can be really tough, especially for older adults. Recall the words of seventy-nine-year-old social worker Renee Solomon whom you read about in chapter 6: "When I walk down the street, nobody notices me any more, and I like to be noticed. . . . In the field and at meetings where I am known, I am listened to because of my credibility. I don't know if that would be true if I wasn't known and people only saw me as an old person."

One person who is unlikely to find herself on the bench or on the shelf is Betty Funk whose profile appears in chapter 9. (Recently I saw her on a local cable television station confidently barreling through the particulars of a budgetary report to town officials.) In Betty's profile, I said she exemplifies traits Malcolm Gladwell describes in *The Tipping Point* by deftly linking people and resources and helping to make things happen. Gladwell, a staff writer for the *New Yorker* and author of another runaway bestseller, *Outliers*, likes to take the measure of accomplished and exceptional people. He wants to know what makes them tick and he is curious about why and how they make things happen and why they are so successful. "It's those who lie outside ordinary experience who have the most to teach us," he finds. He also says that we need to look at the culture, community, family, and generation of people who go far in the world if we are to understand them.[2]

I propose we consider an accomplished and exceptional woman with a remarkable work ethic for the pièce de résistance of this study. I would like to introduce Clara Apodaca, former First Lady of New Mexico. At seventy-six and going strong, this self-made woman qualifies for outlier status, not only because of her age, but also because of her extraordinarily lengthy, varied, and successful careers. Her story is so inspirational and her impact is so extensive, her profile just had to be included. I think you will agree.

PROFILE: CLARA APODACA

Former first lady of New Mexico Clara Apodaca, a trim seventy-six, is the president and CEO of the National Hispanic Cultural Center Foundation. Her job is to raise funds for the Center's many projects, programs, and buildings, and to grow the endowment. The NHCC preserves and promotes Hispanic arts, humanities, and achievements over the past four hundred years.

The leading advocate for contemporary authors, poets, artists, and scholars in New Mexico, the National Hispanic Cultural Center (NHCC) operates under the state umbrella: the state pays for salaries and upkeep, the foundation funds programs and productions.

NHCC's fifty-one-acre campus in Albuquerque boasts three exhibition spaces for visual arts and three theaters in the Roy E. Disney Performing Arts Center (Albuquerque's newest theater), educational facilities, a world-class genealogy library, a restaurant, and a museum store called La Tiendita. Programming includes film premieres, operas, gala balls, art shows, and flamenco festivals. Educational programs for children are free.

The center was intentionally located in the underserved and economically depressed Barelas neighborhood close to downtown Albuquerque in hopes of breathing new life into the community. There are now new restaurants, shops, and tourist attractions in this revitalized area.

NHCC celebrated its tenth anniversary last October with the MARAVILLA 2010 Gala, featuring a golf fiesta and a free community-wide celebration—parade, open house, hands-on art, dance classes, and the unveiling of a 4,000 square foot fresco depicting more than 3,000 years of Hispanic history. Recently however, after nearly a decade of nonstop success in fundraising, the NHCC Foundation has begun to feel the effects of the recession. Clara hasn't lost any foundation sponsors, yet they are all giving less these days. With state funding just as iffy, no new building projects for the NHCC are being planned. The foundation has had to furlough a few staff members and there is less money available for cultural events.

When Clara joined the NHCC Foundation in 2006, she immediately began putting in sixty-hour weeks. "My schedule is incredibly full of lunch and dinner meetings!" She has always worked (since age fourteen), still enjoys it, and finds it makes her happy. However, these days she is no longer in it for the money, it's more about giving back to the community. "In her own humble way my mother instilled middle class values in my sister and me. She taught school in Las Cruces for more than forty years. She was a single parent—my dad died when I was seven years old—and Mom exposed us to music, theater, and the arts, the museum at the university, things most Hispanic kids in the *barrio* never knew about. Mom was also active in her church and volunteered for the March of Dimes, proving the old saying that 'the busiest people are the ones who volunteer first.'"

Clara also looked up to her older sister, Esther, who retired as assistant superintendent of schools in the Albuquerque system. Clara calls her sister the "brilliant one" in the family. When they were small, Esther was double-promoted because in those years the Las Cruces schools did not have a gifted program. "Esther was always four years ahead of me in school but only twenty-one months older! She was smart, had such integrity and was my shining example. She always had my back and still does today. She became my best friend and confidant."

It was hard to follow in Esther's footsteps, though—she graduated from high school at the age of fifteen with a four-point average, then earned highest honors in college. When Clara came along, teachers and professors would exclaim, "Oh, you are Esther's sister. Do you know how smart she was in this English class?" Ever straightforward, Clara says, "I was the average student, cheerleader, and homecoming queen. I had the personality and she had the brains. But we never competed against each other. She was always so proud of my small accomplishments. She was certainly my mentor and is still my best friend and advisor."

Clara also remains close to her girlhood friends from Las Cruces. Most of her older friends who are retired play bridge or golf as a steady diet, but that's not for Clara. She needs to be more active. "I think of myself as 'the new fifty-five' and I feel young inside!" she confides. She has enjoyed her independence following a very difficult divorce fourteen years ago after forty years of marriage. Family comes first—her five children and ten grandchildren—then her job and her relationship with the man she refers to as her gentleman friend. "It can't be all work or all family. A full life means all three," she asserts.

Clara attended New Mexico State University, married early, and had those five children in just seven years. While raising her kids, she worked in the family insurance business and on her husband's successful campaigns for state senator and then governor. Before long, Clara discovered that she was a "political junkie." "I've always been pretty organized, good at remembering names, aggressive about details and keeping track of everything. Plus I always speak my mind. How else could I run a busy household and manage campaigns?"

When her husband was elected governor of New Mexico in 1975 and she became First Lady, Clara decided to focus her energies on the arts and on New Mexico's cultural heritage. Finding that there were absolutely no works of art on the walls of the State Capitol Building in Santa Fe, she set about establishing the Governor's Art Gallery for displaying the work of New Mexico-based artists. Georgia O'Keefe's paintings were the first to be shown; the famed artist herself opened the exhibition. Soon there were also lunch hour concerts in the State House Rotunda.

Clara served as New Mexico's Secretary of Cultural Affairs under two governors in the late 1980s, endeavoring to extend Santa Fe's more plentiful cultural resources to Albuquerque and other parts of the state. She then spent eighteen years in Washington, D.C., working first as general assistant to the chair of the Democratic National Committee, then in the Clinton administration as senior advisor to the Secretary of the Treasury. After leaving the Clinton administration in January 2001, Clara was a consultant for three different organizations and the D.C. mayor appointed her to the Commission on the Arts and Humanities. It was at the Treasury Department that she started an internship program. Mentoring comes naturally to her, as she frequently interacts with many younger business people. "I'm a driver," she laughs. "No matter how hard I push young people to do their best, they consider it a privilege to work for me!"

Has Clara's community spirit and drive rubbed off on her children? Some of them are very active in community service. For example, her son Jeff Apodaca, who had cancer as a youth, founded the Celebration of Life Fund to give college scholarships to fellow cancer survivors. He also provided the funds to create the Jeff Apodaca Multi-Media Center at the University of New Mexico Cancer Center. Clara serves as chairman of the Jeff Apodaca Celebration of Life Foundation.

It's no wonder that a woman who gives so much to her community, her state, and her culture would be honored by all three. For example, *Hispanic Business* magazine selected Clara as one of "100 Influentials" in 2008. Think New Mexico, a "nonpartisan, results-oriented think tank" that develops and advocates for workable solutions to New Mexico's problems, appointed her to the board of directors, as did the New Mexico Women's Forum. National Jewish Health, a medical research and education institute, bestowed the 2010 Spirit of Achievement award for community service on her. And in November 2010 Clara was honored by the Wheels Transportation Museum at a gala fundraiser for development of the Albuquerque Rail Yards in the very same historic Barelas neighborhood that is home to the NHCC. Clearly, what goes around comes around.

When Gladwell was writing about outliers, he also observed that you can find patterns in the lives of successful people when you look closely. Clara Apodaca may be an outlier in some respects, but her story exemplifies many of the interesting patterns uncovered by my study of older professional women, such as following in a mentor's or role model's footsteps, feeling young (at least *inside*), wanting to be active and make a contribution, and enjoying the independence associated with earning a salary. Gladwell would say that Clara has gone far in the world largely because of her allegiance to culture, community, and family. The values and work ethic she absorbed from her mother, a schoolteacher, and father, a farmer and filling station operator, from her older sister, and later from university professors, have sustained her through job challenges and personal setbacks. Like so many of us, she is busy; but more than that, she is using her social skills and political savvy to help make the arts, especially the work of New Mexico's artists, accessible to young and old in Albuquerque, across her state, and beyond.

The stories of the women whom I got to know through this study are filled with both joys and doubts. They speak proudly of what they have achieved in terms of education, work, and family life. They do their best to make time for reading, cultural activities, recreation, fitness, and community service. They are deservedly pleased, but not smug, about their accomplishments, for the roads they traveled have not all been smooth. There may have been false starts along the way, such as taking the wrong educational path, choosing the wrong career, or marrying the wrong guy. There may be discomfort with constantly changing technologies. There may be a growing awareness of being out of step, especially with younger folks' lifestyles, and worry over becoming "invisible" and no longer "counting." Above all, most really love what they are doing—it is stimulating, it is integral to who they are. And, who they are seems quite well defined, even as they leave room for the possibility of more self-discovery in the future. Therefore, they plan to continue working as they age, no matter the income level, no matter the number of hours per week. While retirement remains a desired choice for many women generally, as the

United States is seeing an increase in the number of older working women, the profiles in this book vivify the conversation about this discrete group and illustrate the reasons why they remain in the workforce.

It helps that most are professionals whose jobs can be challenging but do not require them to perform physically demanding tasks beyond their capability. Those who are older and self-employed or consulting enjoy the greatest degree of independence and flexibility. Some of the older women who are employees complain of an occasionally negative climate at work; however, most do not experience adverse working conditions. Still, many admit to bouts of uncertainty about when they will eventually retire, if ever. They know that good health and stamina are essential to performing their jobs. How long they can hold on to good health is anyone's guess. And then there is the bigger picture—when the nation's economy will recover its vigor, and to what extent, remains problematic for everyone. In these hard times, being well educated and having an interesting job that pays relatively well in a field in which jobs are relatively secure enables an older career woman to choose whether and how much to work or to retire. Also having a spouse or partner contributing to household income provides even greater latitude for making that decision. Of course these statements describe ideal life circumstances unavailable to many older women, professionals and nonprofessionals alike, for whom employment is a function of necessity rather than choice.

Gloria Steinem urges women to come together to tell their "personal truth" and hear their experiences confirmed by other women's life stories.[3] My intention in writing this book was to provide an opportunity for older women to do just that, albeit in a reading mode, via the profiles and comments of an especially impressive array of highly competent and hard-charging women. I hope that *Women Still at Work: Professionals over Sixty and on the Job* helps readers discover other career women all across the country who share their determination to continue working as long as they want.

Notes

CHAPTER 1

1. Susan Trausch, *Groping toward Whatever, or How I Learned to Retire [Sort Of]* (Hingham, Mass.: Free Street Press, 2010).

2. US Bureau of Labor Statistics, "Older Workers—Are There More Older People in the Work Place?" (July 2008). The projected increase in working women who are sixty-five or older between 2008 and 2018 (89.8 percent, or 2,030,000 women) will be greater than any other age group. The second highest projected increase (61.4 percent, or 336,000), though smallest in actual numbers, is for working women aged seventy-five years and older. US Bureau of Labor Statistics, "Women at Work." (March 2011).

3. The Associated Press, "Unemployment Rose in 43 States Last Month," National Public Radio. Washington, D.C., January 22, 2010.

4. Sabrina Tavernise, "Recession Study Finds Hispanics Hit the Hardest," *New York Times*, July 26, 2011, A1, A12.

5. Pew Economic Policy Group, "A Year or More: The High Cost of Long-Term Unemployment," April 6, 2010.

6. Re-employment rates for workers ages fifty-five to sixty-four and sixty-five years and older were 39 percent and 23 percent in January 2010 compared with re-employment rates over 50 percent for younger workers. US Bureau of Labor Statistics, "Worker Displacement: 2007–09," August 2010.

7. Sudeep Reddy and Joe Light, "Job Market Picks Up, But Slowly," *Wall Street Journal*, April 3, 2010, A1, A4.

8. Tamara Keith, "Unemployment Pushes Workers into Early Retirement," National Public Radio, April 28, 2010. The average age for retirement has dropped steadily since the mid-1940s when it was close to 70 for men and 68.5 for women. In 2008 it was 63.6 for both men and women.

9. Susannah R. Ottaway, "Introduction: Authority, Autonomy, and Responsibility among the Aged in the Pre-Industrial Past," in *Power and Poverty: Old Age in the Pre-Industrial Past*, ed. Susannah R. Ottaway, L. A. Botelho, and Katharine Kittredge (Westport, Conn.: Greenwood Press, 2002), 9.

10. David F. Warner, Mark D. Hayward, and Melissa A. Hardy, "The Retirement Life Course in America at the Dawn of the Twenty-first Century," *Population Research and Policy Review* 29, no. 6 (2010): 893–919.

CHAPTER 2

1. The Pew Research Center says this is a stereotype and an increasing number of older Internet users (ages fifty to sixty-four) are linking in to social networking sites. Mary Madden, "Older Adults and Social Media," Pew Research Center August 27, 2010.

2. Gail Sheehy, *New Passages: Mapping Your Life across Time* (New York: Random House, 1995), 395.

3. Sheehy, *New Passages*, 356.

4. Gloria Steinem, *Doing Sixty and Seventy* (San Francisco: Elders Academy Press, 2006), xxi.

5. Steinem, *Doing Sixty and Seventy*, 11–12, 46.

6. Marlys Harris, "Forever Young," *Money* (September 13, 2007).

7. Eric D. Beinhocker, Diana Farrell, and Ezra Greenberg, "Why Baby Boomers Will Need to Work Longer." McKinsey Global Institute, November 2008, http://www.mckinseyquarterly.com.

8. Andrew D. Eschtruth, Steven A. Sass, and Jean-Pierre Aubry, "Employers Lukewarm about Retaining Older Workers," Series 10, Work Opportunities for Older Americans, Center for Retirement Research, Boston College (May 2007), 1–9.

9. Ruth Helman, Craig Copeland, and Jack VanDerhei, "The 2011 Retirement Confidence Survey: Confidence Drops to Record Lows, Reflecting 'the New

Normal.'" *EBRI Issue Brief, no. 355.* Employee Benefit Research Institute (March 2011).

10. Melissa Brown, Kerstin Aumann, Marcie Pitt-Catsouphes, Ellen Galinsky, and James T. Bond, "Working in Retirement: A 21st Century Phenomenon" (Sloan Center on Aging and Work and the Families and Work Institute, Boston College, Chestnut Hill, Mass., July 2010).

11. Marc Freedman, *Encore: Finding Work That Matters in the Second Half of Life* (New York: PublicAffairs/Perseus Books, 2007).

12. Brown, et al., "Working in Retirement."

13. The full retirement age is sixty-five for people born in 1937 or earlier. For people born in 1938 or later, it increases gradually until it reaches sixty-seven for people born after 1959.

14. Employee Benefit Research Institute, "The 2009 Retirement Confidence Survey: Economy Drives Confidence to Record Lows; Many Looking to Work Longer." *EBRI Issue Brief #328.* Washington, D.C., April 2009; EBRI and Mathew Greenwald and Associates, Inc. "Age Comparisons among Workers." 2009 RCS Fact Sheet.

15. National Institute on Retirement Security. Washington, D.C. (January 14, 2009).

16. Mark Miller, "Best Remedy for Retirement Security: Don't Retire," Tribune Media Services, 2008.

17. US Bureau of Labor Statistics, "The Baby Boom Generation to Remain in the Labor Force," December 31, 2009.

18. US Bureau of Labor Statistics, "Projected Growth in Labor Force Participation of Seniors, 2006–16," The Editor's Desk, July 31, 2008.

19. Craig Copeland, "Labor Force Participation Rates of the Population Age 55 and Older: What Did the Recession Do to the Trends?" *EBRI Notes.* Washington, D.C: Employee Benefit Research Institute, February 2011. www.ebri.org; US Bureau of Labor Statistics, "Labor Force Characteristics by Race and Ethnicity, 2009," Report 1026, August 2010.

20. Nancy Gibbs, "What Women Want Now," *Time,* October 14, 2009.

21. Catherine Rampell, "Women Now a Majority in American Work Places." *New York Times,* February 6, 2010.

22. Louis Menand, "Books as Bombs—Why the Women's Movement Needed *The Feminine Mystique,*" *New Yorker,* January 24, 2011.

23. Mark D. Constantine, "Captain the Ship," in *Wit and Wisdom: Unleashing the Philanthropic Imagination.* New York: Emerging Practitioners in Philanthropy, May 2009, 98.

24. Constantine, "Captain the Ship," 107.

25. Gail Collins, *When Everything Changed: The Amazing Journey of American Women from 1960 to the Present* (New York: Little, Brown and Co., 2009).

26. Collins, *When Everything Changed,* 352.

27. Collins, *When Everything Changed,* 365.

28. Daphne Merkin, "The Aspirational Woman or Can Anybody Make a Movie for Women?" *New York Times Magazine,* December 20, 2009, 34–36.

29. Lisa Belkin, "The New Gender Gap," *New York Times Magazine,* September 30, 2009.

30. US Bureau of Labor Statistics, "Median Weekly Earnings in First Quarter 2011 by Demographics," April 25, 2011, retrieved from www.bls.gov/opub/ted/archwomen.htm.

31. US Bureau of Labor Statistics, "Women in the Labor Force: A Databook (2011 Edition)," Report 1034, 2011.

32. US Bureau of Labor Statistics, "Women in the Labor Force: A Databook (2010 Edition)" (Table 27. Working Poor: Poverty Status of People in the Labor Force for 27 Weeks or More by Age, Sex, Race, and Hispanic or Latino Ethnicity, 2008), 2010.

33. Retrieved December 13, 2009, from http://graypanthers.org/index .php?option=com_content&task=blogcategory&id=7&Itemid=49; Retrieved December 13, 2009 from http://en.wikipedia.org/wiki/Maggie_Kuhn.

34. The Gray Panthers also advocate continual reauthorization of the Older Americans Act, which supports services to poor, needy, and elderly Americans and provides them with a community service employment program. The act was first passed in 1965; the most recent reauthorization was in 2006. According to the National Health Policy Forum at George Washington University, the act established the Administration on Aging and state agencies on aging to address older Americans' social services needs, help them be independent in their homes and communities, and care for the vulnerable elderly population.

35. See http://owl-national.org; www.wiseolderwomen.com.

CHAPTER 3

1. Susannah R. Ottaway, "Introduction: Authority, Autonomy, and Responsibility among the Aged in the Pre-Industrial Past," in *Power and Poverty: Old Age in the Pre-Industrial Past*, ed. Susannah R. Ottaway, L. A. Botelho, and Katharine Kittredge (Westport, Conn.: Greenwood Press, 2002), 1–12.

2. Anne Kugler, "Women and Aging in Transatlantic Perspective," in *Power and Poverty: Old Age in the Pre-Industrial Past*, ed. Susannah R. Ottaway, L. A. Botelho, and Katharine Kittredge (Westport, Conn.: Greenwood Press, 2002), 67–85.

3. Paul A. Fideler, *Social Welfare in Pre-Industrial England: The Old Poor Law Tradition* (Basingstoke, England: Palgrave Macmillan, 2006).

4. AFL-CIO Department for Professional Employees, "Professional Women: Vital Statistics," Fact Sheet 2009, http://www.dpeaflcio.org/programs/factsheets/fs_2009_Professional_Women.htm.

5. Jacquelyn B. James, Jennifer E. Swanberg, and Sharon P. McKechnie, "Generational Differences in Perceptions of Older Workers' Capabilities," *Issue Brief* 9 Boston College, Sloan Center on Aging and Work, November 2007, 2.

6. Kenneth Gergen and Mary Gergen, "Positive Aging: Sustaining the Vision," *Positive Aging Newsletter* 18 (2003).

7. Marc Freedman, *Prime Time: How Baby Boomers Will Revolutionize Retirement and Transform America* (New York: PublicAffairs/Perseus Books, 1999).

8. James, et al., "Generational Differences."

9. Ron Zemke, Claire Raines, and Bob Filipczak, *Generations at Work: Managing the Clash of Veterans, Boomers, Xers, and Nexters in Your Work Place* (New York: AMA COM/American Management Association, 1999).

10. John Norton, "The Experience Factor," *Education Week*, vol. 29, no. 14, December 9, 2009.

11. Althea Chang, "Fired for Being Old?" *MainStreet Newsletter*, December 3, 2009, http://www.mainstreet.com/slideshow/career/age-bias-work.

12. AARP, *American Business and Older Employees: A Summary of Findings* (Washington, D.C.: AARP, 2000).

13. Michael Winerip, "Generation B," *New York Times*, Sunday Styles, March 7, 2010, 2.

14. Paula Rayman, Kimberly Allshouse, and Jessie Allen, "Resiliency amidst Inequity: Older Women Workers in an Aging United States," in *Women on the Front Lines: Meeting the Challenge of an Aging America*, ed. Jessie Allen and Alan Pifer (Washington, D.C.: Urban Institute Press, 1993), 145.

15. Becca R. Levy and Mahzarin R. Banaji, "Implicit Ageism," in *Ageism: Stereotyping and Prejudice against Older Persons*, ed. T. D. Nelson (Cambridge, Mass.: MIT Press (2002), 49–75.

16. David Neumark, "How Is the Age Discrimination in Employment Act Working? A Look Back and into the Future," *PPI In Brief, No. 139*, Washington, D.C.: AARP Public Policy Institute, June 2008.

17. Laura Hurd Clarke, *Facing Age: Women Growing Older in Anti-Aging Culture* (Lanham, Md.: Rowman & Littlefield, 2011).

18. Margaret Cruikshank, *Learning to Be Old: Gender, Culture, and Aging*, 2nd ed. (Lanham, Md.: Rowman & Littlefield, 2009).

19. Patrick McGeehan, "Study Shows Jobless Rate Varies Widely across City," *New York Times*, December 30, 2009, A23.

20. Michael Luo, "In Job Hunt, Even a College Degree Can't Close the Racial Gap," *New York Times*, December 1, 2009, A1, A4.

21. Alicia A. Munnell and Steven S. Sass, *Working Longer: The Solution to the Retirement Income Challenge* (Washington, D.C.: Brookings Institution Press/Center for Retirement Research at Boston College, 2008).

22. National Institute on Aging, NIH, "An Aging World: 2008," report by Kevin Kinsella and Wan He, available at www.census.gov/prod/2009pubs/p95-09-1.pdf.

23. Dante Ramos, "A Life Worth Living," *Boston Globe*, April 15, 2010. http://www .boston.com/bostonglobe/editorial_opinion/oped/articles/2010/04/15/a_life_worth_ living.

24. Ramos, "A Life Worth Living."

25. Experience Corps, "Fact Sheet on Aging in America" (Washington, D.C.: Experience Corps, 2000).

26. Mary Catherine Bateson, *Composing a Further Life: The Age of Active Wisdom* (New York: Knopf, 2010).

27. Marc Freedman, *Prime Time: How Baby Boomers Will Revolutionize Retirement and Transform America* (New York: PublicAffairs/Perseus Books, 1999).

28. Sheehy, *New Passages.*

29. Sara Lawrence-Lightfoot, *The Third Chapter: Passion, Risk, and Adventure in the 25 Years after 50* (New York: Farrar, Straus and Giroux, 2009).

30. Marc Freedman, *Encore: Finding Work That Matters in the Second Half of Life* (New York: PublicAffairs/Perseus Books, 2007).

31. Lawrence-Lightfoot, *The Third Chapter,* 57.

32. Lawrence-Lightfoot, *The Third Chapter,* 58.

33. James, et al., "Generational Differences," 1.

34. MetLife, "Study of Employee Benefits Trends: Findings from the 8th Annual National Survey of Employers and Employees" (New York: Metropolitan Life Insurance Company, 2010).

35. James, et al., "Generational Differences," 1.

36. Ke Bin Wu, "Sources of Income for Older Persons, 2006" (Washington, D.C.: AARP Public Policy Institute, 2008).

37. Richard W. Johnson and Mauricio Soto, "50+ Hispanic Workers: A Growing Segment of the U.S. Workforce" (Washington, D.C.: AARP, 2009).

CHAPTER 4

1. US Bureau of Labor Statistics, "The Employment Situation—March 2010," Current Employment Statistics. Economic News Release, http://www.bls.gov/news .release/archives/empsit_04022010.htm.

2. US Bureau of Labor Statistics, "Women in the Labor Force: A Databook (2011 Edition)," Report 1034 (2011).

3. Motoko Rich, "Weighing Costs, Companies Favor Temporary Help," *New York Times,* December 20, 2010, A1.

4. Maria Heidkamp, Nicole Corre, and Carl E. Van Horn, *The New Unemployables: Older Job Seekers Struggle to Find Work During the Great Recession* (Boston: Sloan Center on Aging and Work/Boston College and Heldrich Center for Work Force Development/Rutgers University, 2010).

5. Sara E. Rix, "The Employment Situation, September 2010: Older Workers Have Little to Cheer about Once Again." Fact Sheet No. 204 (Washington, D.C.: AARP Public Policy Institute, 2010).

6. Rix, "The Employment Situation," 5.

7. US Bureau of Labor Statistics, "Household Data Annual Averages, 2010."

8. US Bureau of Labor Statistics, "Older Workers—Are There More Older People in the Work Place?" July 2008.

9. Mitra Toossi, "Employment Outlook: 2008–18: Labor Force Projections to 2018: Older Workers Staying More Active," US Bureau of Labor Statistics, *Monthly Labor Review*, November 2009, 33.

10. Wan He, Manisha Sengupta, Victoria A. Velkoff, and Kimberly A. Debarros, *65+ in the United States: 2005*, US Census Bureau, Current Population Reports, P23-209 (Washington, D.C.: US Government Printing Office, 2005), 1. After the baby boomers there is a baby bust cohort born between 1965 and 1975 that will temporarily slow growth, followed by a baby boom echo (a.k.a. Generation Y or the Millennial Generation) born between 1976 and 2001 that will speed it up again, reports Mitra Toossi in the November 2009 *Monthly Labor Review*, US. Bureau of Labor Statistics.

11. He, et al., *65+ in the United States: 2005*.

12. Paula Rayman, Kimberly Allshouse, and Jessie Allen, "Resiliency amidst Inequity: Older Women Workers in an Aging United States," in *Women on the Front Lines: Meeting the Challenge of an Aging America*, edited by Jessie Allen and Alan Pifer (Washington, D.C.: Urban Institute Press, 1993), 133–66.

13. Toossi, "Employment Outlook: 2008–18."; This increase can be compared to a share of the workforce measuring approximately 20 percent in 2009 and 13 percent ten years earlier.

14. Andrew Sum, Joseph McLaughlin, Sheila Palma, Jacqui Motroni, and Ishwar Khatiwada (December 2008), "Out with the Young and In with the Old: US Labor Markets 2000–2008 and the Case for an Immediate Jobs Creation Program for Teens and Young Adults" (Boston, Mass.: Northeastern University Center for Labor Market Studies, December 2008), 5. Retrieved January 27, 2010, from http://www.clms.neu.edu.

15. Toossi, "Employment Outlook: 2008–18."

16. He, et al., *65+ in the United States: 2005*.

17. Toossi, "Employment Outlook: 2008–18."

18. Patrick Purcell, "Older Workers: Employment and Retirement Trends," Congressional Research Service, CRS Report for Congress, RL30629, September 16, 2009.

19. US Bureau of Labor Statistics, "Women at Work," Spotlight on Statistics, March 2011.

20. Selected data adapted from Toossi, "Employment Outlook: 2008–18."

21. Toossi, "Employment Outlook: 2008–18."

22. US Bureau of Labor Statistics. "Older Workers—Are There More Older People in the Work Place?" Spotlight on Statistics, July 2008. (Note figures 1 through 5 are drawn from this US Bureau of Labor Statistics report.)

23. US Bureau of Labor Statistics, "Highlights of Women's Earnings in 2008, Report 1017," July 2009.

24. Sunhwa Lee and Lois Shaw, "Gender and Economic Security in Retirement" (Washington, D.C.: Institute for Women's Policy Research, D456, 2003), 9.

25. US Bureau of Labor Statistics, "Older Workers," Spotlight on Statistics, July 2008.

CHAPTER 5

1. US Bureau of Labor Statistics, "Women in the Labor Force: A Databook (2011 Edition)," Report 1034, 2011.

2. US Bureau of Labor Statistics, "Older Workers—Are There More Older People in the Work Place?" Spotlight on Statistics, July 2008.

3. US Census Bureau, "FM-3. Average Number of Own Children under 18 Per Family, By Type of Family: 1955 to Present," Current Population Survey, 2010 and Earlier.

4. According to a March 2011 BLS report on "Women at Work—Labor Force by Educational Attainment, 1970–2010," 66.7 percent of women (ages twenty-five to sixty-four) in the labor force had some college or a college degree by 2010, compared with just 22.1 percent in 1970. Also see chapter 4, figure 3.

5. Personal income from work does not include Social Security benefits a woman may be receiving.

6. According to Report 1034 of the US Bureau of Labor Statistics, "Women in the Labor Force: A Databook (2011 Edition)," women accounted for 52 percent of all persons employed in management, professional, and related occupations in 2010.

7. Amy Caiazza, April Shaw, and Misha Werschkul, "Women's Economic Status in the States: Wide Disparities by Race, Ethnicity, and Region," 5th Series (Washington, D.C.: Institute for Women's Policy Research, 2004).

8. Greg Mortenson, *Stones into Schools* (New York: Penguin Group, 2009).

9. The National Opinion Research Center's (NORC) General Social Survey of 2002 found that more than half of surveyed Americans strongly agreed or agreed that both spouses should contribute to household income. Only 15 percent agreed with that statement in 1988. Based at the University of Chicago, the NORC General Social Survey is an ongoing study of labor, family, and finances across generations.

10. US Bureau of Labor Statistics, "Employment Characteristics of Families Summary, 2010," Economic News Release, March 24, 2011.

11. Approximately 9 percent of women in the "sandwich generation" (ages forty-five to fifty-six) provide significant amounts of caring for both their dependent children and their aging parents. Charles R. Pierret, "The 'Sandwich Generation': Women Caring for Parents and Children." US Bureau of Labor Statistics, *Monthly Labor Review*, September 2006, 4.

12. Gail Sheehy, *New Passages: Mapping Your Life across Time* (New York: Random House, 1995), 17.

13. Sheehy, *New Passages*, xii–xiii.

14. Sheehy, *New Passages*, 355.

15. Sheehy, *New Passages*, 13.

16. Sheehy, *New Passages*, 361.

CHAPTER 6

1. According to the US Bureau of Labor Statistics March 2011 report on "Women at Work," employment of women in education and health today surpasses the number employed in trade, transportation, and utilities, and in local government.

2. Elizabeth Pope, "Matching Life Experience with New Careers," *New York Times* Special Section on Retirement, March 4, 2010, F1, F9.

3. Unemployment rates across all occupations were higher in February 2010 than one year earlier in 347 of 372 metropolitan areas. US Bureau of Labor Statistics. "Metropolitan Area Employment and Unemployment—February 2010, Economic News Release. Unemployment rates in some of those same areas had improved somewhat by July 2011: they were lower than a year earlier in 257 of the 372 metro areas, higher in 94 areas, and unchanged in 21 areas. US Bureau of Labor Statistics, "Metropolitan Area Employment and Unemployment—July 2011" Economic News Release.

4. Benjamin Cover, "A Comparison of Occupational Employment and Wages in Metropolitan Areas and Nonmetropolitan Areas," US Bureau of Labor Statistics, Occupational Employment Statistics, May 2004.

5. Mauri Elbel, "Working after Retirement Can Offer Fulfillment and Financial Security," *Austin Statesman*, August 22, 2010, Jobs Plus section.

6. Steven Greenhouse, "The Job You Make: Older Workers Mine Their Skills and Connections to Go Their Own Way," *New York Times*, March 4, 2010, F1, F8.

7. Catherine Schine, *The Three Weissmanns of Westport* (New York: Farrar, Straus and Giroux, 2010).

8. Among employed women of all ages in 2010, 27 percent usually worked part time compared with 13 percent of employed men, according to the 2011 US Bureau of Labor Statistics Report 1034 on "Women in the Labor Force."

9. Society for Human Resource Management, "2010 Employee Benefits: Examining Employee Benefits in the Midst of a Recovering Economy" (Alexandria, Va.: Society for Human Resource Management, 2010).

CHAPTER 7

1. Charles V. Willie and Jolene Lane, "Paternal Mentoring Models," in *A New Look at Black Families*, 6th ed., edited by Charles V. Willie and Richard J. Reddick (New York: Rowman & Littlefield, 2010).

2. Willie and Lane, "Paternal Mentoring Models," 132, 140.

3. Jere Longman, "Her Rules, Her Record," *New York Times*, February 15, 2011, B11, B12.

4. W. Chan Kim and Renee Mauborgne, *Blue Ocean Strategy: How to Create Uncontested Market Space and Make Competition Irrelevant* (Boston, Mass.: Harvard Business School Publishing, 2005).

5. Gina Kolata, "Taking Early Retirement May Retire Memory, Too," *New York Times*, Science Times, October 12, 2010, D1, D6.

6. David Carr, *New York Times Book Review*, March 21, 2010, 1, 10.

CHAPTER 9

1. Phyllis Korkki, "Volunteering? It's Easy to Avoid the Waiting List," *New York Times*, November 29, 2009, Bus2.

2. Malcolm Gladwell, *The Tipping Point: How Little Things Can Make a Big Difference* (New York: Little, Brown and Co., 2002).

3. Society for Neuroscience, "Brain Plasticity and Alzheimer's Disease," *Research & Discoveries*. Retrieved March 1, 2010, from http://www.sfn.org/skins/main/pdf/rd/alzheimers_disease.pdf.

4. John Hanc, "In America's Gym, More Than a Touch of Gray." *New York Times*, March 4, 2010, F7.

5. Jane Brody, "Even More Reasons to Get a Move On," *New York Times*, March 2, 2010, D7.

CHAPTER 10

1. Sue Monk Kidd and Ann Kidd Taylor, *Traveling with Pomegranates: A Mother-Daughter Story* (New York: Viking, 2009), 141–42.

2. Malcolm Gladwell, *Outliers: The Story of Success* (New York: Little, Brown and Co., 2008).

3. Gloria Steinem, *Doing Sixty and Seventy* (San Francisco: Elders Academy Press, 2006).

Bibliography

AARP. *American Business and Older Employees: A Summary of Findings.* Washington, D.C.: AARP, 2000.

AFL-CIO Department for Professional Employees. "Professional Women: Vital Statistics." Fact Sheet 2009. Retrieved February 18, 2010, from http://www .dpeaflcio.org/programs/factsheets/fs_2009_Professional_Women.htm.

Associated Press. "Unemployment Rose in 43 States Last Month." Washington, D.C., National Public Radio (January 22, 2010). Retrieved January 27, 2010, from http://www.npr.org/templates/story/stroy.php?storyId=122860486.

Bateson, Mary Catherine. *Composing a Further Life: The Age of Active Wisdom.* New York: Knopf, 2010.

Beinhocker, Eric D., Diana Farrell, and Ezra Greenberg. "Why Baby Boomers Will Need to Work Longer." McKinsey Global Institute. November 2008. Retrieved January 19, 2011, from http://www.mckinseyquarterly.com.

Belkin, Lisa. "The New Gender Gap." *New York Times* (September 30, 2009). Retrieved February 10, 2010, from http://www.nytimes.com/2009/10/04/ magazine/04FOB-wwln-t.html?_r=1.

Brody, Jane. "Even More Reasons to Get a Move On." *New York Times* (March 2, 2010), D7.

Brown, Melissa, Kerstin Aumann, Marcie Pitt-Catsouphes, Ellen Galinsky, and James T. Bond. "Working in Retirement: A 21st Century Phenomenon." Chestnut

Hill, Mass., Boston College, Sloan Center on Aging and Work and the Families and Work Institute (July 2010). Retrieved December 13, 2010, from http:// familiesandwork.org/site/research/reports/workinginretirement.pdf.

Caiazza, Amy, April Shaw, and Misha Werschkul. "Women's Economic Status in the States: Wide Disparities by Race, Ethnicity, and Region." 5th Series. Washington, D.C.: Institute for Women's Policy Research, 2004. Retrieved November 21, 2009, from http://www.iwpr.org/pdf/R260.pdf.

Carr, David. *New York Times Book Review* (March 21, 2010), 1, 10.

Chang, Althea. "Fired for Being Old?" *The MainStreet Newsletter* (December 3, 2009). Retrieved February 10, 2010, from http://www.mainstreet.com/slideshow/ career/age-bias-work.

Clarke, Laura Hurd. *Facing Age: Women Growing Older in Anti-Aging Culture.* Lanham, Md.: Rowman & Littlefield, 2011.

Collins, Gail. *When Everything Changed: The Amazing Journey of American Women from 1960 to the Present.* New York: Little, Brown and Co., 2009.

Constantine, Mark D. "Captain the Ship," in *Wit and Wisdom: Unleashing the Philanthropic Imagination.* New York: Emerging Practitioners in Philanthropy (May 2009) www.epip.org.

Copeland, Craig. "Labor Force Participation Rates of the Population Age 55 and Older: What Did the Recession Do to the Trends?" *EBRI Notes.* Washington, D.C.: Employee Benefit Research Institute, February 2011. www.ebri.org.

Cover, Benjamin. "A Comparison of Occupational Employment and Wages in Metropolitan Areas and Nonmetropolitan Areas." US Bureau of Labor Statistics. Occupational Employment Statistics, May 2004. Retrieved October 3, 2011, from http://www.bls.gov/oes/2004/may/met.pdf.

Cruikshank, Margaret. *Learning to Be Old: Gender, Culture, and Aging.* 2nd ed. Lanham, Md.: Rowman & Littlefield, 2009.

Elbel, Mauri. "Working after Retirement Can Offer Fulfillment and Financial Security." *Austin Statesman* (August 22, 2010), Jobs Plus section.

Employee Benefit Research Institute. "The 2009 Retirement Confidence Survey: Economy Drives Confidence to Record Lows; Many Looking to Work Longer." *EBRI Issue Brief #328.* Washington, D.C.: Employee Benefit Research Institute, April 2009. Retrieved February 3, 2010, from http://www.ebri.org/publications/ib/ index.cfm?fa=ibdisp&content_id=4226.

Employee Benefit Research Institute and Mathew Greenwald. "Age Comparisons among Workers." 2009 RCS Fact Sheet. Washington, D.C.: Employee Benefit Research Institute, 2009. Retrieved February 3, 2010, from http://www.ebri.org/files/FS-04_RCS-09_Age.FINAL.pdf.

Eschtruth, Andrew D., Steven A. Sass, and Jean-Pierre Aubry. "Employers Lukewarm about Retaining Older Workers." Series 10, Work Opportunities for Older Americans. Center for Retirement Research, Boston College, May 2007. Retrieved November 14, 2009, from http://www.bc.edu/centers/crr.

Experience Corps. *Fact Sheet on Aging in America.* Washington, D.C.: Experience Corps, 2000. Retrieved April 14, 2010, from http://www.experiencesorps.org/research/factsheet.html.

Feiffer, Jules. *Backing into Forward: A Memoir.* New York: Random House, 2010.

Fideler, Paul A. *Social Welfare in Pre-Industrial England: The Old Poor Law Tradition.* Basingstoke, England: Palgrave Macmillan, 2006.

Freedman, Marc. *Encore: Finding Work That Matters in the Second Half of Life.* New York: PublicAffairs/Perseus Books, 2007.

———. *Prime Time: How Baby Boomers Will Revolutionize Retirement and Transform America.* New York: PublicAffairs/Perseus Books, 1999.

Gergen, Kenneth, and Mary Gergen. "Positive Aging: Sustaining the Vision." *Positive Aging Newsletter, 18* (2003). Retrieved March 29, 2010, from http://www.taosinstitute.net/resources/pa/?m=200301&cat=4.

Gibbs, Nancy. "What Women Want Now." *Time* (October 14, 2009), 2. Retrieved December 2, 2009, from http://www.TIME.com/time/specials/packages/printout/0,29239,1930277_1930145_193030.

Gladwell, Malcolm. *Outliers: The Story of Success.* New York: Little, Brown and Co., 2008. www.gladwell.com.

———. *The Tipping Point: How Little Things Can Make a Big Difference.* New York: Little, Brown and Co., 2002.

Greenhouse, Steven. "The Job You Make: Older Workers Mine Their Skills and Connections to Go Their Own Way." *New York Times* (March 4, 2010).

Hanc, John. "In America's Gym, More Than a Touch of Gray." *New York Times* (March 4, 2010), F7.

Harris, Marlys. "Forever Young." *Money Magazine* (September 13, 2007). Retrieved December 10, 2009, from http://cnnmoney.printthis.clickability.com/pt/cpt?action =cpt&title=Baby+boomer+survey.

He, Wan, Manisha Sengupta, Victoria A. Velkoff, and Kimberly A. Debarros. *65+ in the United States: 2005.* US Census Bureau, Current Population Reports, P23-209. Washington, D.C.: US Government Printing Office, 2005.

Heidkamp, Maria, Nicole Corre, and Carl E. Van Horn. *The New Unemployables: Older Job Seekers Struggle to Find Work during the Great Recession.* Boston: Sloan Center on Aging and Work/ Boston College and Heldrich Center for Work Force Development/Rutgers University, 2010.

Helman, Ruth, Craig Copeland, and Jack VanDerhei. "The 2011 Retirement Confidence Survey: Confidence Drops to Record Lows, Reflecting 'the New Normal.'" *EBRI Issue Brief no. 355.* Employee Benefit Research Institute (March 2011). www.ebri.org.

James, Jacquelyn B., Jennifer E. Swanberg, and Sharon P. McKechnie. "Generational Differences in Perceptions of Older Workers' Capabilities," *Issue Brief 9.* Boston College, Sloan Center on Aging and Work (November 2007).

Johnson, Richard W., and Mauricio Soto. "50+ Hispanic Workers: A Growing Segment of the US Workforce." Washington, DC: AARP, 2009. Retrieved July 5, 2011, from http://assets.aarp.org/rgcenter/econ/hispanic_workers_09.pdf.

Keith, Tamara. "Unemployment Pushes Workers into Early Retirement." National Public Radio (April 28, 2010). Retrieved from http://www.npr.org/templates/ story/story.php?storyId=126314707.

Kidd, Sue Monk, and Ann Kidd Taylor. *Traveling with Pomegranates: A Mother-Daughter Story.* New York: Viking, 2009.

Kim, W. Chan, and Renee Mauborgne. *Blue Ocean Strategy: How to Create Uncontested Market Space and Make Competition Irrelevant.* Boston, Mass.: Harvard Business School Publishing, 2005.

Kolata, Gina. "Taking Early Retirement May Retire Memory, Too." *New York Times,* Science Times (October 12, 2010), D1, D6.

Korkki, Phyllis. "Volunteering? It's Easy to Avoid the Waiting List." *New York Times* (November 29, 2009), Bus2.

Kugler, Anne. "Women and Aging in Transatlantic Perspective." In *Power and Poverty: Old Age in the Pre-Industrial Past.* Edited by Susannah R. Ottaway, L. A. Botelho, and Katharine Kittredge. Westport, Conn.: Greenwood Press, 2002.

Lawrence-Lightfoot, Sara. *The Third Chapter: Passion, Risk, and Adventure in the 25 Years After 50.* New York: Farrar, Straus and Giroux, 2009.

Lee, Sunhwa, and Lois Shaw. "Gender and Economic Security in Retirement." Washington, D.C.: Institute for Women's Policy Research, D456, 2003, 9. Retrieved April 19, 2010, from www.iwpr.org.

Levy, Becca R., and Mahzarin R. Banaji. "Implicit Ageism." In *Ageism: Stereotyping and Prejudice against Older Persons.* T. D. Nelson, ed. (pp. 49–75). Cambridge, Mass.: MIT Press, 2002.

Longman, Jere. "Her Rules, Her Record." *New York Times* (February 15, 2011), B11, B12.

Luo, Michael. "In Job Hunt, Even a College Degree Can't Close the Racial Gap." *New York Times* (December 1, 2009), A1, A4.

Madden, Mary. "Older Adults and Social Media." Pew Research Center (August 27, 2010). Retrieved October 12, 2010, from http://pewinternet.org/Reports/2010/Older-Adults-and-Social-Media.aspx.

McGeehan, Patrick. "Study Shows Jobless Rate Varies Widely across City." *New York Times* (December 30, 2009), A23.

Menand, Louis. "Books as Bombs: Why the Women's Movement Needed *The Feminine Mystique.*" *New Yorker* (January 24, 2011).

Merkin, Daphne. "The Aspirational Woman or Can Anybody Make a Movie for Women?" *New York Times Magazine* (December 20, 2009).

MetLife. "Study of Employee Benefits Trends: Findings from the 8th Annual National Survey of Employers and Employees." New York: Metropolitan Life Insurance Company, 2010. Retrieved November 29, 2010, from http://www.metlife.com/assets/institutional/services/insights-and-tools/ebts/Employee-Benefits-Trends-Study.pdf.

Miller, Mark. "Best Remedy for Retirement Security: Don't Retire." Tribune Media Services (2008). Retrieved December 10, 2009, from http://www.whatsnext.com/content/best-remedy-retirement-security-don't-retire.

Mortenson, Greg. *Stones into Schools.* New York: Penguin Group, 2009.

Munnell, Alicia A., and Steven S. Sass. *Working Longer: The Solution to the Retirement Income Challenge.* Washington, D.C.: Brookings Institution Press/Center for Retirement Research at Boston College, 2008.

National Health Policy Forum. Washington, D.C. (October 8, 2009). Retrieved February 2, 2010, from http://www.nhpf.org/Library/the-basics/Basics_OlderAmericansAct_10-08-09.pdf.

National Institute on Aging, National Institutes of Health. "An Aging World: 2008," report by Kevin Kinsella and Wan He, available at www.census.gov/prod/2009pubs/p95-09-1.pdf. Retrieved December 15, 2009, from http://www.nia.nih.gov/ResearchInformation/ExtramuralPrograms/BehavioralAndSocial.

National Institute on Retirement Security. Washington, D.C. (January 14, 2009). Retrieved February 3, 2010, from http://www.nirsonline.org/index.php?option=content&task=view&id=172.

National Opinion Research Center. General Social Survey, 2002. Retrieved December 15, 2009, from http://www.norc.org/Research/Topics/Pages/economics.aspx.

Neumark, David. "How Is the Age Discrimination in Employment Act Working? A Look Back and into the Future." *PPI In Brief, No. 139*. Washington, D.C.: AARP Public Policy Institute (June 2008). Retrieved November 20, 2009, from http://star.aarp.org/starweb/researchcenter/servlet.starweb?path=researchcenter/rcmore.fa.

Norton, John. "The Experience Factor." *Education Week 29* (14) (December 9, 2009), 28–29.

Ottaway, Susannah R. "Introduction: Authority, Autonomy, and Responsibility among the Aged in the Pre-Industrial Past." In *Power and Poverty: Old Age in the Pre-Industrial Past*. Edited by Susannah R. Ottaway, L. A. Botelho, and Katharine Kittredge. Westport, Conn.: Greenwood Press, 2002.

Pew Economic Policy Group. "A Year or More: The High Cost of Long-Term Unemployment." (April 6, 2010). Retrieved April 17, 2010, from http://www.prnewswire.com/news-releases/pew-study-nearly-a-quarter-of-all-unemployed.

Pierret, Charles R. "The 'Sandwich Generation': Women Caring for Parents and Children." US Bureau of Labor Statistics. *Monthly Labor Review* (September 2006), 4. Retrieved April 21, 2010, from http://www.bls.gov/opub/mlr/2006/09/art1full.pdf.

Pope, Elizabeth. "Matching Life Experience with New Careers." *New York Times* (March 4, 2010), Special Section on Retirement, F1, F9.

Purcell, Patrick. "Older Workers: Employment and Retirement Trends." Congressional Research Service, CRS Report for Congress, RL30629 (September

16, 2009). Retrieved January 25, 2010, from http://assets.opencrs.com/rpts/ RL30629_20090916.pdf.

Ramos, Dante. "A Life Worth Living." *Boston Globe* (April 15, 2010). http://www .boston.com/bostonglobe/editorial_opinion/oped/articles/2010/04/15/a_life_ worth_living.

Rampell, Catherine. "Women Now a Majority in American Work Places." *New York Times* (February 6, 2010), A10.

Rayman, Paula, Kimberly Allshouse, and Jessie Allen. "Resiliency amidst Inequity: Older Women Workers in an Aging United States." In *Women on the Front Lines: Meeting the Challenge of an Aging America*, Jessie Allen and Alan Pifer, eds. Washington, D.C.: Urban Institute Press, 1993, 145.

Reddy, Sudeep, and Joe Light. "Job Market Picks Up, But Slowly." *Wall Street Journal* (April 3, 2010), A1, A4.

Rich, Motoko. "Weighing Costs, Companies Favor Temporary Help." *New York Times* (December 20, 2010), A1.

Rix, Sara E. "The Employment Situation, September 2010: Older Workers Have Little to Cheer about Once Again." Fact Sheet No. 204. Washington, D.C.: AARP Public Policy Institute, 2010. Retrieved January 18, 2011, from http://www .globalaging.org/pension/us/2010/Employ_Situation.pdf.

Schine, Catherine. *The Three Weissmanns of Westport.* New York: Farrar, Straus and Giroux, 2010.

Sheehy, Gail. *New Passages: Mapping Your Life across Time.* New York: Random House, 1995.

Society for Human Resource Management. "2010 Employee Benefits: Examining Employee Benefits in the Midst of a Recovering Economy." Society for Human Resource Management: Alexandria, Va., 2010. Retrieved February 5, 2011, from http://www.shrm.org/Research/SurveyFindings/Articles/Documents/10-0280%20 Employee%Benefits%20Survey%Report-FNL.pdf.

Society for Neuroscience. "Brain Plasticity and Alzheimer's Disease." *Research & Discoveries.* Retrieved March 1, 2010, from http://www.sfn.org/skins/main/pdf/rd/ alzheimers_disease.pdf.

Steinem, Gloria. *Doing Sixty and Seventy.* San Francisco: Elders Academy Press, 2006.

Sum, Andrew, Joseph McLaughlin, Sheila Palma, Jacqui Motroni, and Ishwar Khatiwada. "Out with the Young and In with the Old: U.S. Labor Markets 2000–2008 and the Case for an Immediate Jobs Creation Program for Teens and Young Adults." Boston, Mass.: Northeastern University Center for Labor Market Studies, December 2008, 5. Retrieved January 27, 2010, from http://www.clms .neu.edu.

Tavernise, Sabrina. "Recession Study Finds Hispanics Hit the Hardest." *New York Times* (July 26, 2011), A1, A12.

Toossi, Mitra. "Employment Outlook: 2008–18. Labor Force Projections to 2018: Older Workers Staying More Active." US Bureau of Labor Statistics. *Monthly Labor Review* (November 2009). Retrieved February 1, 2010, from http://www.bls .gov/opub/mlr/2009/11/art3full.pdf.

Trausch, Susan. *Groping toward Whatever, or How I Learned to Retire [Sort Of].* Hingham, Mass.: Free Street Press, 2010.

US Bureau of Labor Statistics. "The Baby Boom Generation to Remain in the Labor Force." (December 31, 2009). Retrieved March 21, 2011, from http://data.bls.gov/ cgi-bin/print.pl/opub/ted/2009/ted_20091231.htm.

———. "Employment Characteristics of Families Summary, 2010." Economic News Release. (March 24, 2011). Retrieved September 28, 2011, from http://www.bls .gov/news.release/famee.nr0.htm.

———. "The Employment Situation—March 2010." Current Employment Statistics. Economic News Release. Retrieved April 16, 2010, from http://www.bls.gov/news .release/archives/empsit_04022010.htm.

———. "Highlights of Women's Earnings in 2008, Report 1017." (July 2009). Retrieved March 12, 2010, from www.bls.gov/cps.

———. "Household Data Annual Averages (2010)." Retrieved September 27, 2011, from ftp://ftp.bls.gov/pub/special.requests/lf/aat3.txt.

———. "Labor Force Characteristics by Race and Ethnicity, 2009." Report 1026 (August 2010). Retrieved July 4, 2011, from www.bls.gov/cps/cpsrace2009 .pdf.

———. "Median Weekly Earnings in First Quarter 2011 by Demographics." (April 25, 2011). Retrieved July 4, 2011, from www.bls.gov/opub/ted/archwomen .htm.

———. "Metropolitan Area Employment and Unemployment—February 2010." Economic News Release. Retrieved April 21, 2010, from http://www.bls.gov/news .release/archives/metro_04072010.pdf.

———. "Metropolitan Area Employment and Unemployment—July 2011." Economic News Release. Retrieved September 28, 2011, from http://www.bls.gov/ news.release/archives/metro_08312011.pdf.

———. "Older Workers—Are There More Older People in the Work Place?" (July 2008). Retrieved March 12, 2010, from http://www.bls.gov/spotlight/2008/older_ workers.

———. "Projected Growth in Labor Force Participation of Seniors, 2006–16." The Editor's Desk. (July 31, 2008). Retrieved July 4, 2011, from http://data.bls.gov/ cgi-bin/print.pl/opub/ted/2008/jul/wk4/art04.htm.

———. "Women at Work." Spotlight on Statistics. (March 2011). Retrieved March 21, 2011, from http://data.bls.gov/cgi-bin/print.pl/spotlight/2011/women/home .htm.

———. "Women in the Labor Force: A Databook (2010 Edition)." Table 27. Working Poor: Poverty Status of People in the Labor Force for 27 Weeks or More by Age, Sex, Race, and Hispanic or Latino Ethnicity, 2008. (2010). Retrieved July 4, 2011, from http://data.bls.gov/cgi-bin.print.pl/cps/wlftable27-2010.htm.

———. "Women in the Labor Force: A Databook (2011 Edition)." Report 1034 (December 2011).

———. "Worker Displacement: 2007–09 (August 2010)." Retrieved November 1, 2010, from http://www.bls.gov/news.release/pdf/disp.pdf.

US Census Bureau. "FM-3. Average Number of Own Children under 18 Per Family, By Type of Family: 1955 to Present." Current Population Survey, 2010 and Earlier. Retrieved September 28, 2011, from http://www.census.gov/population/ socdemo/hh-fam/fm3.xls.

Warner, David F., Mark D. Hayward, and Melissa A. Hardy. "The Retirement Life Course in America at the Dawn of the Twenty-first Century." *Population Research and Policy Review, 29*(6), (2010): 893–919.

Willie, Charles V., and Jolene Lane. "Paternal Mentoring Models" (February 2010). In *A New Look at Black Families*, 6th ed., Charles V. Willie and Richard J. Reddick, eds. New York: Rowman & Littlefield, 2010.

Winerip, Michael. "Generation B." *New York Times* (March 7, 2010), Sunday Styles, 2.

Wu, Ke Bin. "Sources of Income for Older Persons, 2006." Washington, D.C.: AARP Public Policy Institute, 2008. Retrieved July 5, 2011, from http://assets.aarp.org/rgcenter/econ/fs143_income.pdf.

Zemke, Ron, Claire Raines, and Bob Filipczak. *Generations at Work: Managing the Clash of Veterans, Boomers, Xers, and Nexters in Your Work Place.* New York: AMA COM/American Management Association, 1999.

Discussion Questions

To the Japanese older residents represent an economic force, a pool of talent, "a mountain of treasures." In Japanese society, the elderly can enjoy *ikigai* or "a life worth living." What constitutes a "good" old age or a life worth living in this country?

There are many are different nicknames for the generational cohorts—some researchers call those born before 1946 Traditionalists, followed by the Baby Boom (1946–1964), Generation X (1965–1980), and Generation Y (born since 1980). Others employ slightly different terms: Veterans (1922–1943), Boomers (1943–1960), Xers (1960–1980), and Nexters (1980–2000). Do you appreciate being categorized in this way?

Older women cite various reasons for continuing in the paid workforce past the conventional age of retirement. They might say that they need the income and the health benefits that come with the job. They might say that they get satisfaction from helping others, making a difference, or using their skills and abilities. What factors influence your thinking about retiring versus continuing in the paid workforce? If the economy were not in such dire straits, would you choose to continue working?

Aftereffects of the Great Recession that began in December 2007 are still being felt today. In what ways has the recession affected your life and your work?

Women who continue working in their senior years are often surrounded by much younger colleagues in the workplace. Some of the women profiled in *Women Still at Work* are not bothered by this in the least; others say that it gives them pause. What should older women do to fit in—in terms of their attire, hair style, and conversation?

The seventy-nine-year-old therapist who is profiled in chapter 6 says, "Ageism is more subtle than sexism. When I walk down the street, nobody notices me any more, and I like to be noticed. In the field and at meetings where I am known, I am listened to because of my credibility. I do not know if that would be true if I was not known and people only saw me as an old person." How prevalent is age stereotyping today? Have you experienced it?

The same woman also states that a woman has to fight for her place when she is aging. She thinks that older men have it easier in terms of maintaining their "place" in society. Do you agree with her that men have it easier? Why or why not?

Many older women recall having to choose among a few "female-friendly" occupations for their life's work in the years before the Feminist Movement helped to open up educational, training, and career opportunities for women. Were you steered into secretarial work, teaching, social work, or nursing or did you choose another career path?

Time out for child rearing often delayed a woman's entry or reentry into the labor market. Thus, there are many working women who have no intention of retiring before it becomes absolutely necessary. As one interviewee puts it, "Maybe we are holding on because it was so damn hard to get here." Do you experience similar thoughts when you wonder whether you should keep working or retire?

Many older women can point to at least one person who influenced their career choice, perhaps a parent, a colleague, a boss, a professor, a friend, a teacher or counselor who provided encouragement or acted as a role model. Did you have a mentor at any point along your early or later career path and, if so, how important was his or her advice to you?

Corporate law firms commonly mandate retirement for attorneys who have reached a certain age, usually sometime between sixty-seven and seventy. The oft-cited reason for such a mandate is to make room for younger attorneys. Do you think this kind of policy is reasonable? Why or why not?

Older women can call upon years of experience dealing with life's challenges. They are said to possess "mother wit" that could be extremely useful to younger generations. Why is it so difficult for their children and grandchildren to listen?

The ten-year-old who is a whiz when it comes to new technologies dazzles grandma and grandpa with his or her prowess and just as often leaves them feeling hopelessly behind the times. However, technological literacy is essential for performing a significant number of job functions today. Why are some older men and women eager to acquire essential computer skills and others are not?

The older women in this study tend to be avid readers; many participate regularly in one or even two book groups, in libraries, bookstores, and private homes. Why do you think book groups are so popular these days, especially among women?

Why do pejoratives directed at older men and women, such as "over the hill" and "out to pasture," persist?

How do you define "older" when applied to the "older worker"? If a worker is considered older at age forty for hiring purposes, where does that leave people in their sixties, seventies, and eighties? Do you agree that eighty is really the new seventy, or seventy the new sixty, or sixty the new fifty?

In what ways might men's work life stories differ from the stories you have read in *Women Still at Work*?

Index

About the Author

Elizabeth F. Fideler, EdD, is a research fellow at the Sloan Center on Aging and Work at Boston College. She received a doctorate in administration, planning, and social policy from Harvard University. Dr. Fideler has written and presented extensively on aspects of K–12 teacher development and college/university teaching and learning. Prior to becoming a research fellow at the Sloan Center, she conducted research projects at Education Development Center, Inc. Her current research and writing interests focus on older women who choose to continue in the paid workforce beyond conventional retirement age. Dr. Fideler can be reached at lizpaulfideler@mindspring.com and on Facebook.